William Lang Paige Cox

The Scientific Study of Theology

William Lang Paige Cox

The Scientific Study of Theology

ISBN/EAN: 9783337416546

Printed in Europe, USA, Canada, Australia, Japan

Cover: Foto ©Lupo / pixelio.de

More available books at **www.hansebooks.com**

The Scientific Study of Theology.

W. L. PAIGE COX, M.A.,

VICAR OF ST. PETER'S, ROCK FERRY,
AUTHOR OF "PRESENT-DAY COUNSELS."

London:
SKEFFINGTON & SON, 163, PICCADILLY, W.

1893.

TO

MY MOTHER,

TO WHOSE INTELLECTUAL SYMPATHY

I HAVE ALL MY LIFE BEEN INESTIMABLY INDEBTED,

THIS BOOK IS,

WITH MUCH GRATITUDE AND DEEP AFFECTION,

INSCRIBED.

CONTENTS.

CHAPTER I.
WHY THEOLOGY SHOULD BE STUDIED EXACTLY AS THE OTHER SCIENCES ARE STUDIED ... 1

CHAPTER II.
THE SCIENTIFIC STUDY OF THE NATURE OF GOD ... 36

CHAPTER III.
THE SCIENTIFIC STUDY OF THE QUESTION OF THE FUTURE LIFE ... 65

CHAPTER IV.
THE SCIENTIFIC STUDY OF THE MIRACLES OF THE NEW TESTAMENT ... 86

CHAPTER V.
THE SCIENTIFIC STUDY OF THE NATURE AND PRINCIPLES OF WORSHIP ... 121

CHAPTER VI.
WORSHIP *(Continued)* ... 140

Appendix.

THE HOLY LAND AS THE THEATRE OF REVELATION ... 171

Πάντα δοκιμάζετε·
τὸ καλὸν κατέχετε.

" Ce que je demande c'est que nous nous souvenions que, si nous cherchions la vérité religieuse, c'est pour mieux adorer et pour mieux obéir. Je comprends qu'avant de l'avoir reconnue, nous l'examinions en juges, mais le jour où nous la possédons, il faut nous incliner devant elle."—*Bersier*.

The Scientific Study of Theology.

CHAPTER I.

WHY THEOLOGY SHOULD BE STUDIED EXACTLY AS THE OTHER SCIENCES ARE STUDIED.

THERE is nothing of such profound importance to man as to know what his religious beliefs should be. There is no subject about which it so much behoves him to acquire, as far as he can, clear and correct ideas. Yet there is no department of knowledge which is beset with so many difficulties, in regard to which there have been so many differences of opinion, and in the study of which even by the most thoughtful, the most learned, and the most honest of men, there is so great a liability to error. Probably at no period of history were differences of opinion respecting the subject matter of religious belief so strongly marked as at present, and never in the Christian Church was there such great uncertainty among so many persons with respect to one or other of the old Articles of the Christian Faith.

This is traceable to several causes, among the chief

of which, are (1) the remarkable discoveries that have been made during the present century in every branch of physical science—discoveries which are apparently irreconcilable with much that has hitherto been taught on the authority of Divine Revelation ; (2) the application of a minute and rigorous criticism to the reputed authorship, the language, and the subject matter of the different books of the Bible, and (3) the fuller and more accurate knowledge that has recently been acquired respecting ancient history and literature and the principal religions of the world. All this has tended to throw an intensely searching light of criticism on those doctrines of the Christian Religion which have hitherto been unhesitatingly accepted by the majority, and has set many thoughtful persons to question seriously their claims to belief.

Moreover, the indubitable truths which have been arrived at by modern research have been discovered mainly by the inductive method of reasoning. It is by the patient examination of facts that Darwin and others have made their great achievements in science. The modern scientific spirit is a spirit of patient watchfulness in the face of unknown truth, it does not permit the enquirer to make *a priori* assumptions, and then force facts to fit in with these; it rather prompts him to observe and experiment, and from the results of his observations and experiments to deduce general laws. That this is the right method of enquiring into the secrets of Nature, is proved by the unprecedented success which has followed upon its general adoption. Practically, the book of Nature was sealed to man till he commenced to peruse it in this way, and thus not only has our age witnessed numerous discoveries in every branch of physical science, but new sciences have arisen, and a vast increase of knowledge has been obtained in other departments of research, such as history, literature, archæology, philology, and even ethics and metaphysics. All cultivated persons are now trained to reason by this scientific method, as it has come to be called; they instinctively form generalisations from particular instances, instead of prejudging the results of research by *a priori* assumptions, and they fail to see how objective truth in any branch of knowledge can be accurately learnt in any other way. Hence the disturbance of faith which has been remarked upon is not due only to the apparent collision between the doctrines of religion and the truths of science, but also, and perhaps chiefly, to the fact that the doctrines of religion are supposed to lie for the most part outside the scope of a strictly scientific enquiry, so that the method of reasoning which has proved triumphant all along the line of investigation into the works of God in Nature, is set on one side when the subject of study is that department of truth which is called distinctively religious.

The real question at issue between ordinary teachers of dogmatic theology and those who differ from them is the question of how religious truth is to be ascertained. Are matters of religious belief to be subjected to the same treatment as all other matters into which enquiry is made? Is the method which has been found so marvellously successful in tracing out the truth in respect to matters scientific and historical, and in making surer the limits of truth and falsehood, or at any rate of probability or improbability, in matters relating to conduct and the operations of the human mind—is this method to be rejected in the investigation of such matters as the existence of God, His nature, and His will, and the way in which, and the extent to which, men can know Him? About the propriety of following the scientific method in some departments of theological research there is no question. All the best linguistic criticism of the New Testament, in which some English scholars have obtained such creditable success, has been conducted strictly on the lines of scientific enquiry. Ought we, or ought we not, to apply the same method of enquiry in every respect to every part of the Bible, not only to its words but to its composition, to its history, to the events it relates and to the doctrines it enunciates? Again, if the Bible ought to be read in the same way as we all acknowledge the book of Nature and the book of secular history should be read, can any satisfactory reason be shewn why those formularies in which the opinions of the Church in different ages have been expressed, should not be verified by the same method, or at any rate be subjected to the same test? This is the main question at issue between theologians and other scholars, and until it is settled, there is no probability of any general agreement being arrived at amongst thoughtful and cultivated persons with respect to the subject matter of religious belief. As it is at present, very many writers on theology, while affirming theology to be a science, study it and teach it in a different manner from that in which every other science is studied and taught. They lay down beforehand certain axiomatic propositions and deduce their principal doctrines from these, with the result that many of those to whom they address themselves, not assenting to their propositions, look with disfavour upon their doctrines. On the other hand, not a few thinkers who have been trained in the strictly scientific school have examined the doctrines of theology by the scientific method as they have believed, and have arrived at conclusions at variance with those of the theologians, and in some respects altogether subversive of religious belief.

Hitherto, for example, it has been the general practice of theologians to rest the truth of what is called revealed religion on some authority, the authority of the Bible or the Church, or both; and men have been required to believe the doctrines of the Christian religion on one or other of those authorities as being an infallible declaration of the mind of God. Now it is just this deference to an infallible authority, however sacred it may be in name, that reasonable men in these days are not prepared to pay. They find it contrary to the analogy of Nature that there should be any divinely certificated complete and final repository and guarantee of truth, and they are not prepared to assent to the assumption that an exception might be looked for in the case of religious truth. Even supposing that it is of greater importance to men to be rightly informed concerning religious truth than any other kind of truth, it by no means follows from that that it would be in accordance with the Divine plan to provide for men an infallible guide to such truth. And, moreover, even if it were probably in accordance with the Divine will for men to be provided with an infallible guide to religious truth, it is not at all within the limits of our powers to assume beforehand that that infallible guide would take this form or that. We have not more ability to forecast the action of God in any particular case, than we have to forecast the action of men, and the difficulty of doing the latter is proverbial. I may know a man so well as to be fairly sure *how*, that is, from what motives, he will act under certain circumstances, whether generously or ungenerously, prudently or imprudently; but that is a different thing from my being able to foretell precisely *what* he will do. The characters of men are so complex, and their particular actions are determined by such a variety of causes, that it is seldom that I would venture to say that my friend would do exactly this or that. In proportion as my friend was wiser and better informed than I, my conjecture as to his probable conduct would be liable to be erroneous. Now, if there is this impossibility of assuming safely beforehand what any man would do under particular circumstances, how plainly impossible it must be to forecast with perfect certainty what God would do under particular circumstances, how probably different would be His plan of action from what we might conceive it would be!

The prejudice, therefore, against any *a priori* assumption as to the provision by God of some infallible authority upon which men might base their belief of religious truth is well grounded in reason. It is confirmed by experience. There are at least two such assumptions serving as the foundations of different systems of thought among Christians, and the instability of the structure in each case has proved the insufficiency of the foundation.

The Evangelical Protestant has assumed in the past that God would impart certainty to men concerning His truth by giving them an infallible book, a book every word of which was to be read as dictated by God, and every statement in which was stamped with His authority. Recent events must have clearly proved to the most intelligent and open-minded of this school that the Bible is not such a book as they supposed it was, and that there was no warranty in fact for the assumption on which they based its verbal infallibility. It was a very plausible theory this, it seemed to indicate a very natural way for the communication of religious truth to men, it represented God as doing just what we might have expected He would do, but God's ways are not our ways, as we often have painful reason to know.

The assumption of the directly opposite school of Christians is that God would make known to men the certainty of the truth concerning Himself by means of a Society miraculously preserved from error. It is hardly necessary to point out that here we are in the region of pure conjecture, and that there is not a particle of solid ground on which to base the likelihood of the institution of an infallible Church. The whole Romanist position has been so brilliantly and conclusively dealt with by Professor Salmon in his work on the *Infallibility of the Church*, that it is sufficient to refer to that work for a refutation of it. The chapter on " The Blunders of the Infallible Guide," would of itself satisfy any candid mind as to the baseless character of the Roman claims. Inasmuch, however, as an appeal is made to argument for the support of these claims, and they are represented as resting on the authority of certain texts of Scripture, it is worth while just to glance at those texts in order to see how faulty is the chain of reasoning constructed out of them. The chief text is, " Thou art Peter, and upon this rock I will build My Church."* This is a verse found in only one of the Synoptic Gospels, and, in the judgment of some textual critics, is of doubtful authenticity. Nevertheless it is the foundation upon which the whole Biblical argument for the infallibility of the Roman Church is made to stand, as follows—" The Church of Rome was founded by St. Peter," (an assertion of which absolutely no proof can be given, nay, which is directly contrary to the fact : St. Peter may have visited Rome, but he certainly did not found the Church there, it was in existence some time before he first set foot in Italy) "therefore it is the Church of which Christ spoke."

* St. Matt. xvi. 18.

(A manifest *non sequitur*.) "Moreover, the Church" (narrowed to mean the Roman Church) "is of Divine institution, therefore it is infallible." (Another *non sequitur*. "The powers that be are ordained of God," but whoever yet believed that *they* were infallible?) But the Church has a guarantee of its infallibility in the texts—"Lo, I am with you alway, even unto the end of the world:"* and, "When He, the Spirit of Truth, is come, He will guide you into all truth."† Yet how can it be proved that the "you" in these texts refers not to the general body of Christians who are partakers of the Spirit of Truth, but only to the clergy, or rather to the bishops with the Pope at their head; and how can it be shewn that the presence of Christ with His Church is not consistent with the existence of evil within it, and that the promise of guidance into all truth—a gradual process necessarily—implies also the preservation meanwhile from all error? It is difficult to see in such reasoning as this a serious attempt to prop up the monstrous assumption, that one fallible man, assisted by a number of other fallible men, can produce absolutely accurate statements of religious truth.

As little can the position taken up formerly by the Gallican Church, and maintained in substance now by some members of the Church of England, be deemed satisfactory. In this School the belief in the infallibility of the Church is retained, only the infallibility is attributed to the whole Church and not simply to the Roman

---

* St. Matt. xxviii. 20. † St. John xvi. 13.

branch of it. Considering that the whole Church has been hopelessly divided since the first few centuries of the Christian era, the reference to the infallible authority of the Church can only be made with respect to opinions that were held in common by the Fathers of the early Church and to those that were defined in the Creeds.

The unsatisfactory character of this position is demonstrated by the extravagance of the assumption that underlies it, that the Church of the first few centuries was in possession of a gift which has been practically denied to the Church since—an assumption which, as a Roman Catholic controversialist has put it,* really amounts to this, "that the Holy Ghost has failed of His mission during two-thirds of the lifetime of the Church which He was by Divine promise to lead into all truth." Christ's promise to His Church in that view can only be read to mean, "You shall not be led into all truth, you shall not advance further than to what was attained in such and such a century." Moreover, it is quite impossible to shew that the saintly writers of the early Church, much as they may have been illuminated by the Spirit of Truth, were not nevertheless subject to the intellectual limitations of their day. We know for certain that they believed and taught as truths of religion, doctrines such as that of the six days' Creation and the rotation of the sun round the earth, which are now acknowledged to be erroneous, so that if infallible accuracy is to be attributed to such

* Quoted by Salmon. 2nd Ed. p. 278

opinions concerning religious truth as were held by all the early Fathers alike, infallible accuracy ought to be attributed also on the same ground to many exploded errors.

The fact is, there has been a very considerable increase of human learning and of critical power since the early days of Christianity, and it is inevitable that the result of this should be to alter men's views as to the way in which the truths of religion are to be understood. The Church of this age must be in some points wiser than the Church of the Age of the Councils, though on other points it may be not so wise; and directly that is conceded the Gallican theory of infallibility at once breaks down. According to that theory it is maintained that when once the majority of Christians have agreed in a conclusion, that conclusion must never afterwards be called in question. " But why not," as Dr. Salmon asks, " if the Church has in the meantime become wiser? If God, without injustice and without danger to men's souls, can leave many of His people for a considerable time imperfectly informed and even in erroneous opinion as to certain doctrines, what improbability is there that He may have left a whole generation imperfectly or erroneously informed on the same subject, and reserved the perception of the complete truth for their successors ? " *

The full stress of the infallible authority of the Church is laid of course on the three Creeds, which are now taught by some to be verbally infallible in the

* Ibid, page 177.

way that the Bible was formerly taught to be verbally infallible, so that the rejection of the Creeds is now represented to be "a greater bar to Christian fellowship than the rejection of the New Testament itself." There can be no question that the Nicene Creed, having been drawn up by a majority of the Bishops of the Christian Church in the fourth century, has remarkable claims upon the reverential attention of all students of theology, and, as will be pointed out later on, there are good reasons for believing on other grounds that all the articles that compose it are substantially true. But to believe implicitly in the absolute verbal accuracy of the Nicene Creed on the ground of the infallible authority of the Church is really to rest one's faith on the proposition, that the Christians of the fourth century were possessed of a power of defining the truths of religion which was never possessed before and has never been possessed since, a proposition of which no proof can be given, and which is indeed utterly improbable. It may be urged that the authority of the Church in favour of the Creeds gains in weight from the fact of their having been assented to by the majority of Christians in every age of the Church since; but it is clear that they have been assented to on the ground of the belief that those who composed them were divinely preserved from error. Christians of subsequent ages have been unwilling to set their private judgment against the supposed infallible authority of the compilers of the Creeds.

If it is said further that, after all, the compilers of the Creeds merely put together what they found in the Bible and added to it nothing new, the answer is obvious. The terminology which they used was in itself for the most part new, supplied by the philosophy of the day, and it was no slight change to embed the truths of religion in a framework extraneous to the first form of Christianity. From this point of view, therefore, the assertion of the verbal infallibility of the Creeds really amounts to the assertion that the philosophy of the fourth century was exactly fitted to provide a perfect mould of expression for the theological truths contained in the Bible; yet it is surely not self-evident why the philosophy of the fourth century had an advantage in that respect over the more developed and, in many respects, improved philosophy of our own time.

For these and similar reasons the doctrine of "diffusive" Church infallibility, as it is called, is as unsatisfactory a basis for a Christian to rest his faith upon as the doctrine of the infallibility of the Roman branch of the Church.*

Involved as he is in such hopeless perplexity when he listens to what the different schools of Christian thought have to say to him respecting the proper basis of his religious belief, it is not surprising that the man of modern culture should find himself strengthened in

* It may be worth while to point out that this is not to say that there is not *an* authority of the Church. It is the assumption of the *infallibility* of the Church in one form or another that has been found to be improbable, or at any rate useless for practical purposes.

his prejudice against any and every *a priori* assumption as to how God would certify His truth to men. What we have seen of late, therefore, in some quarters is the absolute rejection of every theory of Biblical inspiration and of Church authority, and the subjection of all religious questions to the freest investigation. The result has been a wide-spread scepticism concerning many articles of the Christian Faith. It has been represented either that they have been tried in the ordinary balances of truth and have been found wanting, or that they are without the range of scientific enquiry, so that nothing can with surety be known of them.

Now, apart from all controversy, those articles of the Christian Faith which plainly represent the actual teaching of Christ, and which would be regarded as fundamental by all Christians, and as distinctive of Christianity by all non-Christians, have been the religious mainstay of many thousands of conscientious and thoughtful persons. It can scarcely be denied that hitherto they have inspired the purest morality that has been exhibited on earth, and have afforded the greatest possible encouragement and consolation in labour and sorrow to those who have heartily believed them. Their known practical effect makes it exceedingly improbable that they are in substance false. So that there may be many, who, while sharing the prevalent dissatisfaction with exclusive appeals to authority, whether Biblical or Ecclesiastical, feel nevertheless that the process of reasoning is defective, by which it is contended that the fundamental articles of the

Christian Faith have been shewn to be unworthy of belief. Those who have enquired into them with this result in the name of scientific truth have professed and have thought themselves to have been guided by the scientific method, but it can be shewn that in several particulars they have departed somewhat from those principles which as a rule they undeviatingly adhere to in the study of other branches of knowledge. They have made imperfect inductions by rejecting certain classes of facts which should not be left out of account in the study of theology, they have arbitrarily refused to allow that any other faculty of man than the reasoning faculty can render any assistance towards the discovery or verification of religious truth, they have paid little or no attention to the enlightening power of personal goodness as an aid to the perception of a certain class of truths, and they have made affirmations in the name of science which are demonstrably untrue and unsupported by the evidence of experience.

Instances of such imperfect inductions and ungrounded affirmations will be given later. Meanwhile it may be suggested that the best hope of a final agreement about the subject matter of religious belief is to be looked for in the adoption by all of a common method of enquiry. At present the theologian depends for the demonstration of his conclusions on one style of argument, and his opponent on another, with the result that there is a hopeless misunderstanding between them. That misunderstanding will certainly continue until they find some common ground upon which to base their reasoning, and such common ground can only be found in the agreement to study theology scientifically, in other words, to deal with theology in the same way that every other science has come to be dealt with. Till that is done, not only will theologians stand apart from a large number of students of science, notably of biological and anthropological science, appealing to them in vain for the acceptance of their dogmas, but they will continue to fail of the support of the many who accept the demonstrated facts of science, and who are not nevertheless out of sympathy with the aims of Christian teachers, though they reject some of their dogmas. This is a circumstance that ought to very profoundly impress the Christian theologian, that there is a deeply rooted prejudice against theology in the minds of many thoughtful and cultivated persons, who yet avow themselves Christians. Among not only the special students of science, but the poets, the litterateurs, and the ethical writers of the present day, dogmatic theology is held in but slight estimation. The present style of apologetics may avail somewhat to strengthen the faith of those who acquired their religious opinions apart from the evolution view of the origin of Nature, or who, though generally well-informed, are not fully aware of the extent to which modern discoveries appear to tell against the truth of certain beliefs; but as a means of persuading those whose minds are saturated with modern ideas it is useless. An immense amount of labour and ingenuity in the sphere of Christian apologetics is simply wasted, because it is ineffectual as a means of removing the objections to theology as it is commonly taught, which are entertained by the leaders of modern thought, whose opinions are certain to gain more and more acceptance with the reading public, and through it with all classes of the community. Theologians have then nothing to lose, and probably a great deal to gain, by coming down from their high standpoint of authority and of *a priori* reasoning, and boldly submitting the premisses upon which their arguments are constructed to the test of the inductive method, in the confidence that, as their doctrines are true, the truth of them will be made not the less but the more apparent, when they are investigated by a method which is acceptable to those whom they wish to convince.

Yet it may be objected that it is an impossibility for theology to be placed on a level with the other sciences, since the class of things with which theology deals are not capable of being subjected to scientific scrutiny in the sense in which this is true of the objects of outward Nature. The same objection was till recently supposed to hold good with reference to mental and moral science; but John Stuart Mill has disposed of it by a chain of reasoning which, *mutatis mutandis*, may well be applied to the case of theology. He has shewn[*] that any facts are fitted in themselves to be a subject of science which follow one another according to constant laws, although

[*] *A System of Logic*, Book VI.

those laws may not have been discovered, nor even be discoverable by our existing resources. As yet the state of mental and moral science may not be as satisfactory as might be desired, yet none can deny that by the use of the scientific method of enquiry a great deal has of late been ascertained and a great deal is likely to be still further ascertained in the future respecting the mental nature of man and the laws relating to human conduct. The affinity between theology and ethics, for example, is so close, and the difficulties which beset the study of either science are so similar, that it is not easy to see why the one science is capable of being placed on an inductive footing and not the other.

Yet it may be argued, that, after all, mental and moral science only relates to man while theology relates to God, and that, therefore, though men may best discover by observation and generalisation what is true in regard to human affairs, the method must be ineffectual when applied to the things of God, which are necessarily beyond the scope of ordinary observation. What, for example, could a scientist learn in the ordinary way about the doctrine of the Trinity? Nay, what can be learnt for certain by the scientific method about the very existence of God? Have not some scientists told us that they have "swept the heavens with their telescopes, and found no God?"

The objection is one which shews how great is the difficulty of obtaining *exact* knowledge about the things of God—greater by far than the difficulty of obtaining exact knowledge about the nature of man, and how necessary it is that all the conditions of successful enquiry concerning the nature of God should be complied with, but it holds good for no more than that. It never has been a dogma of theology that man cannot "receive the things of the Spirit of God," but only the natural man. Theology deals with a class of facts which are only discernible and appreciable by those whose intelligence is illuminated by purity of heart. By a strict process of inductive reasoning the theologian can shew that the "things of the Spirit of God" are to be "spiritually judged." In other words, a strong presumption amounting to positive proof can be made out in favour of the reality of certain propositions which are held to be true with a consensus of certitude by men of the very highest spiritual type. It can be shewn that certain facts concerning the nature and will of God are only ascertainable in the first instance by those in whom high intellect is combined with high character, as though the fullest development of a man's mental and moral powers had the effect of opening to him sources of knowledge to which men of less mental and spiritual elevation cannot penetrate. It has been represented hitherto that knowledge so obtained has been acquired by the process of "revelation," *i.e.*, by the unveiling by God to chosen men of truths concerning Himself which common men are not able or worthy to perceive. Whether the term "revelation" fitly expresses the facts of the case will be a matter for subsequent enquiry. It is sufficient now to point out that even if the term is rightly used, if religious knowledge is actually acquired by special communication from God, it is quite possible nevertheless for the truths of religion to be made the subject of inductive enquiry. Even if it were proved that the highest truths are "revealed" there would be every necessity that it should be ascertained exactly what truths are revealed. Even if it were admitted that human knowledge concerning the essential subject matter of religious belief has an extra-ordinary source, yet, inasmuch as men are the instruments by whom this knowledge is conveyed to men, and inasmuch as it has to be conveyed to others by means of speech or writing, it is most demonstrably requisite that the scientific method of reasoning should be employed, in order to distinguish what is pure religious truth from what is not, to eliminate from the statements of the recipient of Revelation those portions which bear the impress of his imperfections, and to discover everywhere the permanent elements of religion beneath the forms in which they are transitorily clothed, so that it may be discerned what is rightly the subject matter of religious belief, and what has usurped its place.

It is on matters of this kind that the gravest mistakes have been made both by theologians and their opponents, and there is no possibility of either arriving at correct conclusions, and so coming to agree with one another, until they both adopt a strictly scientific method of investigating the problems with which theology deals. If they do meet on this common ground, sooner or later they will arrive at the same results. It may be later rather than sooner. Even now, for example, though the theory of evolution has been before the world for upwards of thirty years, there is by no means perfect agreement among biologists as to the process by which different species are produced and perpetuated. It was the opinion of Darwin, and is still that of many, that natural selection is the chief, but not the only, cause of organic evolution, while Mr. Wallace and others believe that natural selection is the sole and only principle which has been concerned in the development both of life and of mind from the amœba to the ape. Still, inasmuch as both the school of Darwin and that of Wallace are working by precisely the same method of investigation, and submit their conclusions to precisely the same kind of proof, there can be little doubt but that eventually they will arrive at the same opinion. Similarly there is every probability that an agreement will be arrived at respecting various doctrines of theology which are now in dispute, when once a common method of investigating them has been adopted ; only, from the greater difficulty of research into theological truth, and the greater complexity of the subject, the time when there will be an agreement as to results is likely to be more distant.

It seems therefore worth while to attempt to lay down one or two principles which should be generally assented to and acted upon in the investigation of the subject matter of religious belief. Discarding all arbitrary assumptions as to the exclusive claims of any kind of authority, and rejecting on the other hand the unscientific prejudgment of different religious questions, it ought to be possible for students of religious truth to arrive at something like a consensus of opinion on such points as the following.

I. The statements of the Bible concerning scientific matters are to be treated in exactly the same way as similar statements in all other books are treated. There is no preponderant weight to be attached to the authority of any ancient book, however sacred, or to the opinions of any class of men, however honest and wise, with respect to matters of scientific fact. The truth or falsehood of all such assertions is to be determined by a comparison of them with the certain results of scientific research, carried on strictly according to the inductive method of reasoning. If, for example, it is conclusively proved by this method that the different forms of animal and vegetable life were not produced in six days, then it is certain that the first chapter of Genesis does not give a scientifically accurate account of the origin of species. If, again, it can be demonstratively shewn that such a thing as the stoppage of the rotation of the earth upon its axis for a period of some hours has never taken place within historic times, then it must be allowed by all that the quotation from the Book of Jasher inserted in the tenth Chapter of Joshua (which quotation, by the way, implies the belief of the author that the sun moved round the earth), does not relate a scientific fact. Of course it may be urged by some, that, seeing that all things are possible with God, it is quite possible that He may have wrought such a stupendous miracle on behalf of a people that He had a special regard for, as to stop the rotation of the earth in order that that favoured people might win a victory over another people. But that objection is not to the point. It would not be seriously questioned by any that all things are *possible* with God. The question at issue between those who believe, and those who do not believe, that the quotation from the Book of Jasher exactly describes an objective fact, is not a question as to whether God *could* make the "sun to stand still," but as to whether He ever *did* such a thing. And the evidence against the alleged occurrence is simply overwhelming. Not only is it not written in the records of the solar system, as science can trace them, but it is clean contrary to all reasonable probability. The authority of a very ancient book written in days when there was no truly scientific knowledge of the order of Nature, and even the authority of thousands of good men who have firmly believed in the story since, have no weight whatever in deciding such a matter. There can be no possibility of any substantial agreement between the theologian and the scientist until it is conceded by the former that the statements of the Bible concerning matters of physical science are to be subjected to the ordinary scientific method of proof. The utmost that the theologian can require is, that in testing the truth of such statements, the scientific method shall be properly used, and that no conclusions shall be drawn with regard to the truth or falsehood of the narrative of an alleged miracle till all the factors have been weighed by means of which such an occurrence might possibly have taken place. It will need a separate chapter to discuss this point, but meanwhile it may be stated that the result of a proper application of the scientific method to the examination of the alleged miracles of the Bible will not be to disprove all the reports of such occurrences, but to give a different explanation of some of them.

II. A second principle that must be assented to by students of religious literature in order that they may pursue their investigations upon common ground is, that questions of literary and historical criticism must be freed from the embargo of authority. There must be no limit to the employment in the study of the Bible of those methods of criticism which have been applied with such fruitful results to other ancient literatures. The student of the Old and New Testaments must not be debarred from certain lines of investigation by any *a priori* assumption as to the inspiration of Holy Scripture or the authorship of certain books. It must be permissible to him to deal freely with one and all of the books of the Bible. He must be authorized to try and discover whether the five books commonly attributed to Moses form a consecutive narrative written by one man, or whether they are a compilation of materials composed at different periods and with different theological and ethical characteristics. He must be allowed to determine, if he can, by internal or external evidence, how many, or if any, of the Psalms were written by David, whether the Book of Isaiah is, or is not, entirely from the hand of the prophet who was contemporary with Hezekiah, and whether in the rendering of certain passages of the Bible the reading of the Septuagint or of the Hebrew text is to be preferred. Moreover, he must be considered at liberty to test the historical statements of the Bible by comparing them with the contemporary records of other nations. In short, the Biblical critic must have a free hand, it being only understood that his criticism must be honest and fair. It must be carried on and its results stated with a regard for the supreme reverence in which the books of the Bible have ever been held, and with a sincere desire to elucidate the truth which they contain. Above all things, the critic must take care that by emulating the humility, the good faith, and the personal holiness of the sacred writers, as they are rightly called, he may be qualified to apprehend their full meaning, and to sympathize with their general aims, it being an indispensable canon of Biblical study, as stated by the author of the *Imitation of Christ* that "each part of Scripture is to be read with the same spirit wherewith it was written." Undoubtedly some free critics of the Bible have failed in this, and in consequence they have not only arrived at erroneous results in their critical researches, but they have excited a just prejudice against themselves on the part of those who from mistaken reverence have deprecated the free and full criticism of the Bible.

It must be added that no criticism of the Bible can be satisfactory or lead to true results, unless a due deference is paid to the opinions current nearest to the time when the Bible was composed, and to the authority of Biblical scholars in the past. There is no deference due to the kind of authority by which it was imposed by a decree of the Council of Trent* on the members of the Roman Church that they should believe that the Epistle to the Hebrews was written by St. Paul; but there is a certain weight to be attached to the fact that at that period there was a widespread opinion among scholars of the Roman Church in favour of the Pauline authorship of that Epistle. Similarly, the modern critic of the Bible cannot do his work in a truly scientific spirit unless he pays a proper regard to the interpretations and the critical statements to be found in the writing of the early Christian Fathers and of the best scholars in each branch of the Church since.

III. A third principle that must be accepted by all students of theology, if there is to be any substantial agreement between them, is the following:—That in the investigation of the subject matter of religious belief very high authority is to be attached to the opinions of men of the most approved wisdom and the most conspicuous purity of life. Religious truth, or what has passed for such, has always been brought to light, not by mere students and philosophers, but by men who have had a peculiar power of discerning it.

* " Testamenti Novi .... quatuordecim Epistolæ Pauli Apostoli, ad Romanos, &c. .... ad Hebræos."

It has not been reasoned out, as is the case with most other kinds of truths, but "seen." Whether this power of "vision," which has always been supposed to characterize those who have added to or purified the knowledge of religious truth, is in part explicable as an abnormal facility for reasoning correctly concerning the deep things of Nature and of human life, may be a debatable question. On the whole, however, there seems good reason for thinking that the word "seeing" rather than the word "reasoning" best describes what actually takes place when a man acquires what has been wont to be called a "revelation." There are certain states of consciousness in which truths hitherto unknown are perceived as by a flash of inward light, just as objects in Nature are suddenly revealed to the outward eye by the light of the sun when it falls upon them, and it seems as reasonable to associate the authorship of the one kind of illumination as of the other, with the Ultimate Source of all things. At any rate, in every case the absolutely essential condition of obtaining such fresh knowledge of religious truth has always been a detachment from selfish and ignoble aims and a desire to be taught by a Power outside one's self, and those who have laid claim to the possession of new religious truth have always asserted that they have not found it out for themselves, but that it has been "revealed" to them. Thus they have established a strong presumption in favour of the opinion that religious truth is in the first instance conveyed to men not by the ordinary processes of knowledge but in some way unknown to us, which cannot be more accurately described than by the name of "revelation." Dealing with the facts as we find them, we are bound to acknowledge that some men have exhibited an exceptional power of ascertaining religious truth, and we cannot fail to observe that there is an inseparable connection between what we are fain to call religious insight and holiness of life. That the facts so conveyed to us are facts, is attested by their adaptability to explain the mysteries of life and to guide conduct. They are accepted as true because they are verified in a most conclusive manner by the experience of thousands. And whatever may or may not be known exactly as to *how* they were first apprehended, it is thus rendered absolutely certain that those who did first apprehend them were possessed of a power of discerning religious truth which ordinary men do not possess, and that, therefore, their authority is entitled to the utmost weight when enquiry is made into any of the matters about which they have made pronouncements.

IV. It must next be agreed that affirmations concerning what is said to have been "revealed," definitions of doctrine, may be legitimately examined, in order that it may be ascertained whether or not they have been correctly argued out, and that even the original products of what is alleged to be revelation are to be tested, as far as possible, by their agreement or disagreement with the indubitable truths which have been brought to light since they were first delivered. The doctrine of the Trinity, for example, is not to be considered beyond the scope of criticism because it has been affirmed by General Councils and has been assented to by a majority of Christians in every age since. It must be recognized as quite reasonably permissible to go behind the Creeds, and to investigate whether or not they accurately embody what is taught in the Bible concerning the Divine Nature. It goes without saying that all the theological opinions, whether set forth in the Creeds or not, which men have professed to have derived from the Bible, concerning such matters as the efficacy of the death of Christ, the nature of the Resurrection, and the future state, must be considered to be credible or not according as they accurately represent the teaching of the Bible, or as they are conformable, when such conformity is possible and may be sought for, with the testimony of science and history, and as they lie within the region of reasonable probability.

Further than this, even the theological teaching of the Bible in every part of it must be held to be a legitimate subject of criticism. Such doctrines as the Fatherhood of God, the Divinity of Christ, and the existence and influence of spiritual beings, are to be examined with reference to the teachings of science (in the broadest sense—not physical science only) and experience, so that it may be ascertained whether there is a reasonable basis for belief in them. It must be understood, however, that the collective opinion of the wise and good in the past must be considered to have a distinct though by no means an infallible authority, on similar grounds to those laid down in the previous section, in determining the truth in respect to those doctrines.

V. It must also be admitted by all serious and fair-minded students of theology that faith is a legitimate factor in the building up of a personal belief in those doctrines of religion which when tested by reason are seen only to lie in the region of the probable. When the choice is put before a man of accepting one of two opposite opinions, neither of which is demonstratively certain, but one of which must be true, and when it is inevitable that he should accept one or the other, it must be acknowledged that it is a reasonable and right thing for him to decide in favour of that which his interest and his better feelings alike incline him to prefer.

VI. All questions relating to religious rites and ceremonies, Church government, and the like, must be finally decided by the test of propriety and utility, and the best criterion of this propriety and utility is afforded by the opinions and customs of Christians since the foundation of the Church, justified as they are, or the reverse, by the verdict of history. The authority of the Church has most weight in matters of ritual and morals, as it rests on such an enormous mass of observed facts and experience in human nature; but the authority of the Church, which is properly the authority of Christian opinion and custom, must not be limited in time or space: the Church whose authority is to be quoted is post-Reformation as well as pre-Reformation, and it is co-extensive with the Christian world. It is evident that an opinion or custom universally prevalent at one period of history loses a certain proportion of the weight of authority in its favour when it has been forcibly protested against at another period.* In this view it will be seen that there is not universal authority—Catholic authority in the proper sense of the word—in favour of episcopacy, because since the Reformation it has not prevailed in every quarter of the Christian world; but there is a preponderance of Christian opinion and custom in favour of it. Similarly, there is a preponderance of authority in favour of the arrangement of the Christian year in the Church of England, as a method of commemorating the chief events in the life of Christ and securing the remembrance of the chief articles of Christian belief.

VII. It is of supreme importance that it should be noted by all, that an earnest desire to seek information in every quarter from which knowledge concerning religious truth can be acquired, and a resolute intention to free oneself from every possible tinge of prejudice, and to cultivate a hearty willingness to discover and duly appreciate truth in whatever form it is to be met with, is indispensably necessary to the successful study of theology. The science of God and the science of human conduct in reference to God must have relation to every science which deals with the works of God and the nature and history of man. The professed theologian cannot, without running the risk of

---

* This is in accordance with the Vincentian rule,—"*quod semper, quod ubique, quod ab omnibus.*"

very serious error, allow himself to be ignorant of the results of the latest research in all the principal departments of science—astronomy, geology, biology, anthropology, and archæology. It is particularly needful that he should be accurately informed concerning the origin and development of religious ideas throughout the world, the history of ecclesiastical institutions, and the evolution of morality, as these matters are treated by those who have made a special study of them.

He is not properly equipped for the service of the "Queen of Sciences" who has not endeavoured to qualify himself for the task by the acquisition of a diversified culture. Still less can theological truth be thoroughly grasped without the most sacred care for accuracy in the study of the subjects which are regarded as belonging to the special province of theology, such as the literary and textual criticism of the Bible, Church history, and Christian literature. Just as no professed theologian can be regarded as properly furnished for his work without possessing a knowledge of all that the scientists can teach him that bears upon the subject of his study, so no person who has been careful to acquire the general culture of the day can be held competent to pronounce judgment on the work of the theologian until he has acquainted himself with all the facts which have shaped the opinions that have formed themselves in the theologian's mind. And none, whatever be the nature and degree of his culture and attainments, can arrive at an accurate perception of particular religious truths or a sense of their value and importance without the experience gained by teaching them to others, or observing the effects either in the way of reproof or encouragement or consolation that they are apt to produce upon men and women of every type of character and intelligence in common life.*

The right study and judgment of religious questions demands then a varied knowledge of science, of history, and of the nature of men, as well as of specially religious literature. Still more imperatively does it require a moral preparation which can only be effected by the earnest and continued effort to live in the performance of what is loving and true. A great deal of the bigotry on the one hand and the intemperate scepticism on the other that are rife at the present day are due to the neglect of this primary condition of successful theological study, not simply to ignorance of truths which are complimentary to others which are clearly perceived, but to want of fairness, want of candour, and an insincere attachment of the cause of truth for its own sake. It may be quite true, as Hooker has remarked,† that " by the bitter strife which riseth oftentimes from small differences of religious belief, and is by so much always

*Perhaps the ideal training for a theologian is to study in a *University* where all the arts and sciences are taught up to date, to pass through a divinity school, and afterwards to engage in parochial work. This was the training of the greatest of English philosophical theologians, Richard Hooker.

"It was a saying of Dr. Arnold, certainly no disparager of intellect, that no student could continue long in a healthy religious state unless his heart was kept tender by mingling with children, or by frequent intercourse with the poor and suffering."
   —J. C. Shairp. *Culture and Religion.* Ed. 1884, p. 90.
† *Ecclesiastical Polity*, Book V., Ch. i. 3.

C

greater as the matter is of more importance, we see a general agreement in the secret opinion of men, that every man ought to embrace the religion which is true, and to shun, as hurtful, whatsoever dissenteth from it;" but it is equally true that "in any controversy the instant we feel angry we have already ceased striving for truth only, and begun striving for ourselves." No doubt the immense issues dependent on the truths of theology, and on the right presentation of them, seem to justify the student of theology in his indignant protests against what he judges to be false, and certainly justify him in his censure of those who treat the science with levity or in a spirit of wilful perversity. And yet only too easily does the personal and even selfish element enter into his indignation. He is contending for doctrines that, as he judges, are of great value to the race, but which are also very precious to himself, and that not simply because his present peace and his highest hopes are, as he supposes, bound up with them, but because they are his doctrines, adopted by him, it may be, after much toil and struggle of head and heart, or because they are the doctrines of the religious society to which he is attached and in whose honour or dishonour he indirectly shares. Thus his zeal for truth is apt to become very largely a zeal for his own interests and his own credit. From such a bias likely to lead to heated defence of one's own opinions, it is exceeding difficult to free one's-self, and yet if the simple willingness to discover truth, and the simple belief in the excellence and the power of truth however brought to light, were, as it should be, the prime motive of the theological student, as it is, say, of the enlightened student of geology, the theologian would be as calm in dealing with those who differ from him as the geologist. The geologist, indeed, cannot claim moral superiority over the theologian on the score of the relative calmness with which he deals with his science, for no such important issues to himself or to others are dependent on the accuracy of his opinions. Nevertheless, until theological questions come to be discussed on either side with the same absence of acrimony which characterises the discussion of matters that are dealt with in the other sciences, it cannot be said that theology is being studied in a truly scientific spirit or in a way that is likely to lead to satisfactory and permanent results.

In the succeeding chapters an attempt will be made to show what conclusions are likely to be arrived at by an application of the scientific method to the investigation of some of the articles of Christian belief that are most controverted at the present day.

CHAPTER II.

GOD.

IN endeavouring to deal in a strictly scientific way with the subject that lies at the foundation of theology, viz., the existence and nature of God, it will be convenient first to review the data which contribute to our knowledge of God, and then to compare the results to which they lead us with what has hitherto been the Christian doctrine on the subject.

We may start from a fact which may be assumed to be acknowledged by all who are entitled to speak with authority on matters scientific or religious, and which may be stated in the words of Mr. Herbert Spencer. "We are obliged," he says, "to regard every phenomenon as a manifestation of some Power by which we are acted upon; .... we are unable to think of limits to the presence of this Power;* .... the certainty that it exists is the certainty towards which intelligence has from the first been progressing."† And again, "One truth must grow ever clearer—the truth that there is an Inscrutable Existence everywhere manifested, to which we can neither find nor conceive

---

* *First Principles.* Ed. 1890, p. 99.　　† Page 108.

either beginning or end. Amid the mysteries which become the more mysterious the more they are thought about, there will remain the one absolute certainty, that we are ever in presence of an Infinite and Eternal Energy, from which all things proceed."* This then is the first unquestionable fact that we have to take into account in setting theology on a scientific basis, that there is "an Inscrutable Power manifested to us through all phenomena, an Infinite and Eternal Energy, from which all things proceed." There is no need to dilate on this proposition by way of proof or explanation. None is concerned to deny it, the orthodox theologian as little as the student of science: it cannot be denied.

It is equally certain that, to utilize the phrase of another writer† who stands without the orthodox camp, there is in the world "a stream of tendency that makes for righteousness." There is no fact which is more capable of scientific verification than this, that all our actions are followed by certain consequences which are exactly proportioned to the nature of those actions. It is quite true, as Mr. Herbert Spencer says, ‡ that "to mentally represent even a single series of those consequences, as it stretches out into the remote future, requires a rare power of imagination; and to estimate their consequences in their totality requires a grasp of thought possessed by none." Still that there are such consequences proceeding from every action,

---

* *Ecclesiastical Institutions.* Ed. 1885, p. 843.
† Matthew Arnold.   ‡ *First Principles,* p. 117.

whether good or bad, is evident to any cultured mind. The subject has been dealt with by recent writers,* who may be referred to as furnishing details and illustrations of it, which could not be supplied here without serious digression from the main argument. As an incontrovertible fact we may couple it with that which has been previously mentioned, and say that the actions of men bring about good and bad consequences "through the established order of the Power that manifests itself through all phenomena."

But these consequences are moral and of the nature of rewards and punishments. Men who do good actions experience good consequences from those actions, and men who do bad actions are visited with evil consequences. True, the good and evil consequences are by no means in every case perceived by those who are affected by them, nor even by others; yet on the whole it is evident to any ordinary observer that the message entrusted to the prophet of old was a true one: "Say ye to the righteous, that it shall be well with them, for they shall eat the fruit of their doings. Woe unto the wicked! it shall be ill with him, for the reward of his hands shall be given him."†

But we can legitimately go a step further than this. It is capable of genuine scientific proof on the lines laid down in the previous chapter, that the discipline of human life, carried on by means of the good and bad

---

* Emerson: *Essay on Compensation*, and F. W. Robertson: *Sermons*, Vol. I. No. 14. See also Bishop Butler: *Analogy*. Pt. I. Chap. 2.
† Isaiah iii. 10, 11.

consequences which follow upon the actions of men, is wholly of a beneficial character to those who submit to it in a penitent, humble, and patient spirit. That men of generally pure life often bear unmerited pains, and have almost an equal share with others of the suffering that is due to natural causes, is of course a truism. But the general consent of the good is that such pains and sufferings do not work them any real harm, that on the contrary they tend to promote their highest well-being. No doubt there will always be a considerable number of persons who will demur to this optimistic view of the function of pain. They will neither concede that pain in their case has, or could have had, such good effects, nor will they allow that it has such good effects on others; or, if they do make any acknowledgment of this kind, they will not suffer the possible beneficial effects of pain to counteract in their minds the depression produced in them by the contemplation of the immense amount of suffering with which human life is charged. Yet, on the whole, the testimony of the thoughtful and pure-minded in favour of the beneficial character of the discipline to which man is subjected in respect of the good and bad consequences which proceed from his actions is strong and clear. We look for such testimony not simply in Christian quarters; we find it in the sacred literature of the East, in Greek philosophy, and in Roman Stoicism. Still it is Christianity that has raised its voice loudest in assertion of the blessed results of pain. It has actually called upon men to rejoice " when they have

fallen into divers trials." It has afforded numerous examples of men, who, instead of shirking pain, have rather courted it, and have exhibited to the world a marvellous spectacle not merely of courageous and
• uncomplaining submission, but of joy in the midst of suffering. Nay more, it has boldly taught that the highest development of character is impossible without the discipline of pain. It has represented its ideal character, as being subject to the necessity of being made " perfect through sufferings."

We have arrived now at this point. There is a Power behind phenomena with which we are forced to associate the maintenance of a system of law controlling human life, the tendency of which is to purify the characters of those who cheerfully submit to it, and to promote the highest well-being of the wise and good. Now, if we desire to describe exactly the nature of this discipline of life, we can only speak of it as parental. It corresponds precisely to the way in which every prudent and conscientious parent tries to order the education of his child. He corrects the child when he has done wrong, encourages him when he has done right, endeavours to be always evenly just in dealing with him, and is not deterred by the fears or entreaties of the child from causing him to undergo present inconvenience in order that he may be spared future pain. The aim he sets before himself is the proper formation of the child's character, and he postpones every other consideration in the interest of the child to that. Very few parents, indeed, realise this aim : so distressed are the majority of parents at the thought of their children suffering, even though temporarily, in mind or body, that they frequently refrain from administering that treatment to their children which is called for in their highest interests. But no such softness is ever discernible in the discipline of life which is carried on in accordance with the immutable law of consequences. It is wholly and in all particulars calculated to perfect character. True, the many, even the majority are not appreciably benefited by it; but none the less does the truth stand, that thus, and thus only, can those who desire to be better than they are, be morally improved. There are failures under this universal discipline of man—the failures outnumber the successes; but yet the system is, so far as we can conceive, the best possible; and though in equity and regularity it far transcends what any earthly parent has ever done for a child, it can only be represented in terms adapted to our experience as parental;—it is the ideal which in our imperfect efforts after the moral education of our children we seek to keep in view.

If the discipline of human life, contrived and ordered by the Invisible Power, is of a paternal character, we are fain to regard that Power with feelings similar to those with which we regard an earthly father, and it is natural and reasonable therefore to speak of the Fatherhood of God. Do we thereby ascribe personality to God? On strictly scientific grounds it is not apparent that we are justified in doing so. The knowledge of God which we possess is not sufficient to empower us to make any affirmations about His essential nature. We can make inferences, legitimate inferences, concerning the purpose which underlies the government of human life; and finding that that government makes for righteousness we can attribute moral qualities to the Author of that government—justice, love, and so forth—just as we can deduce the moral character of a man from his actions. But we have no data for making any positive statements about the essential nature of God. One thing, however, is incontestably certain, that His nature is in every respect higher than that of man. It cannot on any supposition be lower. If personality is a necessary attribute of the highest being, as it certainly differentiates man from the lower animals, then something at least as high as personality must be attributed to God. It is quite inconceivable that man, with his lofty attributes of consciousness, intelligence, and will, can be the product of an utterly insensate and unintelligent Power working blindly towards unknown results. There must be in the Inscrutable Power at least all the capacity which exhibits itself in man through consciousness, intelligence, and will; though it is quite possible, as Mr. Herbert Spencer has argued,* that there is " a mode of being as much transcending intelligence and

---

*First Principles, page 109.

Cf. Principal Shairp, *Culture and Religion*;—" It is because moral law is but a condensed expression for the energy of, shall I say, a *Higher Personality, or something greater, more loving, more all-encompassing than personality, that it comes home to us with the power it does.*"

will, as these transcend mechanical motion." There is no occasion, then, to cling to all that is implied in the phrase, "personality" in order to maintain the dignity and perfection of the Invisible Power. For aught we know, there may be something higher than personality; and a due regard for a purely scientific method of reasoning must restrain us from dogmatizing in this, as in other matters, about what we do not know.

None the less, however, is it true, that the Unknown Power must remain for us a Being with whom we can have no satisfactory religious relations, except we accustom ourselves to think of Him in terms of personality. We may stand in awe of an Inscrutable Power, and will and strive not to sin, lest we should bring upon ourselves the consequences, of self-reproach and pain and loss, which are attached unerringly by that Power to wrong-doing. But prayer is impossible except we address ourselves to Some One—a Father; and without prayer, religion cannot be. In order that our belief in a Supreme Power may afford to us the fullest possible incentive and ability to do right, and consolation under bereavement and suffering, we must pray; and that we may pray, we must approach the Invisible Power as we would a brother man in this respect that we must compel ourselves to think of Him as a Person. We must go through all the forms of thanking Him for our past blessings, of confessing to Him our past sins, and of seeking His guidance and help in the future. Without prayer, in the sense in which the wisest and holiest of Christians have chiefly understood it* as meditative converse with the Invisible Power, we cannot achieve the best possible to us in right doing. The various graces of the highest character can only flourish in an atmosphere of prayer. Would we be truly humble and modest from day to day, we must reflect day by day that we are merely the recipients of the bounty of the Invisible Power, we must recall the various benefits we have received, and return thanks for them. Would we have a proper sense of the meanness, the hatefulness, and the mischievousness of sin, we must call to mind our various acts of sin, and reflect that they are acts of rebellion against the righteous laws of a Being Who has subjected us to a discipline which is wholly paternal. Would we prepare ourselves for future action in such a way that we may do under particular circumstances what is wisest and best, we must seek with all our heart and mind to know what is in accordance with the Will (as we should say, speaking of an earthly personage), of Him in Whom we live, and move, and have our being. And when trouble, or

---

* "We do not use the word prayer (*oraison*) solely as the petition for some good thing, poured out before God by the faithful, as St. Basil defines it, but rather according to St. Bonaventura, who says that prayer (or meditation), generally speaking, includes all the contemplative acts; or St. Gregory Nyssen, who taught that prayer is intercourse of the soul with God; or St. Chrysostom, who calls it a parley with the Majesty of God; or lastly, St. Augustine and St. Damascene, who say that prayer is an uplifting of the mind to God"—St. Francis de Sales. *Of the Love of God* (translated by H. L. Sidney Lear), p. 176.

"Prayer is an exercise of holy thoughts."—Bishop Wilson. *Sacra Privata*.

sorrow, or weakness comes upon us, we must, if we would bear it in the best possible spirit, reflect that it has happened to us in accordance with that Will, and that what that Will ordains or permits cannot eventually do harm to those who submit to it with patience and resignation.

It can thus be scientifically proved that there has been a solid substratum of fact underlying the doctrine of the Christian Church concerning the Fatherhood of God, the Divine Providence, and the efficacy of prayer. With each belief, however, certain opinions have been associated which cannot be verified scientifically, and which have arisen from the abuse of that anthropomorphism which man cannot entirely avoid in his thoughts concerning the Infinite Power. Although it was by a correct instinct that men learnt to think of the discipline of human life by the Supreme Power as paternal, yet they naturally and almost inevitably in an earlier day fell into the mistake of believing that God's action towards men was in every respect like that of an earthly father, except that He never acted unwisely or sinfully. Without going back to the times when it was thought that God actually "repented," "was wroth," etc., it was till quite recently the general belief among Christians that God was such a Being that He changed His disposition towards certain persons, and exerted Himself specially either on their behalf or against them. We know now that His laws operate upon every part of human life with undeviating regularity. We have no reason to believe that they are ever interrupted by the special and extraordinary action of God Himself. In fact, all the evidence we have points the other way. Still, the effects produced upon men by their own actions are such as to make them feel as though God were acting under the influence of certain passions excited by them. When they do wrong, and are reproved for it by their own consciences, it seems as though God were angry with them; when they contravene the moral laws, and lose their health, or their fortunes, or the respect and affection of their friends, it seems as though God Himself were interposing to punish them; when they neglect penitence and prayer, it seems as though God were withdrawing His favour from them; when they confess their faults, and ask for pardon, it seems as though God were forgiving them; and when they busy themselves in some occupation which is plainly in conformity with the Divine laws, or engage themselves in devout meditation on some of the ways in which the benevolence of God is displayed, it seems as though He were smiling upon them, and visiting them with His approbation. We have no authority, as has been said, for thinking that God does change towards us in any such way. It may be so, but we have no ground for thinking it. We stand on a more solid foundation when we conceive of Him (to use a familiar simile) as remaining ever the same, like the sun which at all times shines with undimmed lustre beyond the clouds, that by their presence or absence made the day dark or bright for us. Scientifically, then, we have no justification for thinking that God is, in respect of the method by which He maintains the discipline of human life, "such an one as ourselves;" yet it is difficult for us to express to ourselves the nature of the experiences of which we are conscious when we act in accordance with or in disobedience to His laws, without saying that God smiles upon us, punishes us, or visits us with His displeasure. We have, indeed, experiences which make it *seem* as if we had excited these feelings in the Supreme Power; but they are produced in us by the orderly operation of the Divine laws, and it is only through that orderly operation, so far as we can ascertain the facts, and not through any special interferences on God's part, that the disposition of God towards us at any time is revealed.

Thus the doctrine of the special providence of God, as hitherto generally taught in the Christian Church, seems not to be in accordance with the teaching of science. The facts, as has been frequently said, all point to the uninterrupted operation of the Divine laws. Yet it did stand in men's minds for an indisputable truth, viz :—that every single one of their actions entailed corresponding consequences under the discipline of life carried on by the immutable laws of God, just as though a special interposition had on each occasion been made on their behalf by God. In a word, a scientific observation of the laws which govern human life has taught us that God exercises that influence for the good of men by means of His unchangeable laws, which He was formerly thought to exercise by the special acts of His providence. So that the Christian loses nothing by giving up his literal belief in that doctrine. He rather acquires thereby an increased reason for adoring a God Who does in His majestic unchangeableness what He was formerly thought to do after the fashion of men by repeated efforts of will.

A scientific observation of the facts has also given us a higher conception of the agency of God with respect to prayer. Formerly, in contravention of the frequent warnings in the Bible of the inefficacy of the kind of prayer that is not in accordance with the " Divine Will," men thought of prayer chiefly as an instrument for obtaining the fulfilment of their own wishes; and, moreover, they conceived that, when they asked God to do something for them, the effect was that the orderly operation of the laws of God was interrupted on their behalf. We know now that the operation of the laws of God is never interrupted, even by prayer, and that many requests that men may make are in consequence quite outside the region of prayer. We are no longer able to think of prayer as a kind of force which runs athwart and interrupts the other forces which operate in Nature and on human life, though there is much ground for thinking that it is a force which may take its place among other forces in producing even physical results. At any rate there are some remarkable incidents narrated in the Bible and of more recent occurrence which justify that supposition. There is a ring of scientific truth about the familiar lines,

> " More things are wrought by prayer
> Than this world dreams of." *

Yet we have more definite evidence as to the subjective than the objective effect of prayer; and that is the effect of prayer to which the greatest prominence is given in the Bible, and to which the lives of the Saints bear the most conspicuous witness. None can pray without feeling the better for it, and none can ask for any moral or spiritual benefit without receiving it. Indeed, it is plainly a law of the religious life that our moral and spiritual attainments are in proportion to our devout wishes expressed in prayer, and moreover that the character of our religious life will correspond to the character of our prayers. For example, if we intermingle intercessions with our requests on our own behalf, we shall habitually think of and act for the benefit of others as well as ourselves; if we address thanksgivings to God as well as petitions we shall be nourished in a cheerful and unselfish religion; if we accustom ourselves to recall and confess our faults we shall increase in humility, and so forth. All those precepts in the New Testament relating to prayer, such as "Ask and it shall be given you, etc.," "In nothing be anxious, but in everything by prayer and supplication let your requests be made known unto God," are shown to be absolutely correct from the certain results which follow when they are acted upon. Still it has to be remembered that they are necessarily

* Lord Tennyson, *The Passing of Arthur.*

couched in anthropomorphic language, for how could we find other terms in which to express the nature and operation of prayer? We may not take them to imply that God is moved to extraordinary efforts of will by our words, any more than by our actions. Even the parable of the Unjust Judge, which appears to give the most anthropomorphic representation of God to be found in the Gospels, cannot be read as conveying any true lesson except it be taken to teach that patient persistence in prayer is absolutely necessary to its producing a full and proper effect. We cannot rightly think of God as personally acted upon by importunity like the judge in the parable, nor, indeed, is it stated that He is. The thing emphasized in the parable is the importunity of the widow. Our importunity must be such, and it will have its reward, though the answer it produces will be in accordance with the orderly operation of law; and it will not come as the extraordinary action of a God Who is moved to exert Himself on our behalf on account of His being wearied by our prayers. As Bishop Wilson has said, "Importunity makes no change in God, but it creates in us such dispositions as make us fit to receive our petitions."

The result at which we have arrived is, that the anthropomorphic terms which are used to describe God's agency with respect to the discipline of human life and the effect of prayer express substantial truths, though they have hitherto been commonly understood too literally, and been associated with certain erroneous or at any rate doubtful conceptions concerning the method of the Divine operations.

But we cannot associate the thought of God only with the phenomena that present themselves to our senses in the material world, and with the discipline of human life. The most remarkable by far of the existences in Nature of which we have any knowledge is man. Physically, indeed, we may class him with the lower animals in reference to his formation and preservation by the Supreme Power; but there is something in man which sharply differentiates him from the brutes, and, moreover, which compels us to entertain other thoughts concerning God than those which are suggested to us by the two classes of facts already mentioned, that is to say, those pertaining to the existence and history of the universe, and to the discipline of human life. The most sublime things by far with which we have any acquaintance are the virtues, exhibited in the lives of the best of men,—justice, love, humility, purity, and so forth. These graces of character are not only unspeakably beautiful in themselves as subjects of contemplation, but they are most powerful forces, though immaterial, exerting an immense influence upon human life, adding intensely to its pleasures, and furthering immeasurably the advancement of the race. Whether or not, or how, they have been gradually evolved during the long ages in which man has lived in social intercourse with his fellows, this is not the place to discuss. Anyhow, they now present themselves to us as a class of things of which cognisance must be taken when we are considering our relation to the Supreme Power. If it is true to speak of that Power as "the Infinite and Eternal Energy, from which all things proceed," then these graces of human character must have proceeded ultimately from that source. It is beside the point to argue that the vices of human character must on the same ground have proceeded from the same source; for it can be definitely shown that the vices are of distinctly human origination, and can only be associated with the thought of God's authorship in so far as they are the product of that capability of spontaneous action with which man has been endowed by God. In this respect they stand by themselves, and are not to be compared even with similar actions wrought unthinkingly and without the exercise of choice by the brutes. The virtues are not of human origination in the same sense as the vices, and moreover they cannot be classed with the vices in relation to our experience of the operations of the Supreme Power, inasmuch as the vices exhibit in themselves nothing superior to the other kinds of phenomena of which we have experience, and which have been already referred to. The virtues belong to a higher order of things than any of these, and therefore they unavoidably suggest to our minds other and higher thoughts concerning "the Power by which we are acted upon." Now, if we are justified, as the accredited exponents of Science not only allow but affirm, in regarding all phenomena as a manifestation of that Power, if we have a warranty therefore for inferring that there must be in that Power something at least as high as what we call personality in man, something at least as high as consciousness, intellect, and will, then by the same reasoning it is demonstrable that there must be in God something at least as high as what in man we call a just, loving, pure, humble, and self-sacrificing character. In a word, the Supreme Power must be not only just, loving, etc., but must possess those virtues in the highest degree, and be, as we say, perfect.

There is thus opened to us a kind of knowledge concerning God other than that which we derive from the study of Nature and the contemplation of the course of human affairs. We learn of God from the nature of man, as well as from the environment in which man is placed, and from the consequences which proceed from his actions. But it is not from all men that this testimony arises. Some men exhibit in their conduct so little that is amiable or admirable that they add nothing to what Nature of itself teaches us concerning God. It is only men of a purer type who present to our view in their lives and characters a set of phenomena which afford a new manifestation of the Invisible Power. And of these One, by common consent of all, has so realized in Himself all the highest possibilities of goodness, has so exhibited in His life all the virtues in their fullest development, that in Him as in no one else we see the full moral nature of God revealed. Through Him we have learnt that God is not only all-powerful and just, but is merciful, humble, and self-sacrificing. There may be phenomena which seem to conflict with this moral estimate of the Infinite Power, yet, in His inmost nature He must be what Christ exhibited Himself to be, else there are things in the universe which are of higher and purer quality than the source from which they proceed.

We arrive then by a strictly scientific process of reasoning at the truth, that the Supreme Power is revealed in morally perfect humanity, as well as in Nature and through the discipline of human life. There is that in God which corresponds exactly to the moral character of good men, and especially of Jesus Christ ; and the nature of which that character was the exhibition is of direct Divine authorship. This is the truth which the Christian Church has hitherto proclaimed in its doctrine of the Divinity of Christ. It is a doctrine which has come down to us expressed in the terms supplied by the Greek philosophy which was current in the age of the Councils. It is possible that in the increase of wisdom and knowledge a more perfect expression of that doctrine may hereafter be arrived at. At any rate, in no satisfactory way can it be argued that the decisions of the majorities at certain councils have such weight as to be considered by succeeding ages in every respect infallible. It is an assumption that is wholly untenable in a scientific light that the Christian bishops of the fourth and fifth centuries were possessed of a faculty for defining theological truth which has never since been possessed by Christians. If men now are able to make more exact statements of astronomical and geological truth than it was possible to make in ancient times, so it is only likely that more exact definitions of theological truth may be made in the future. Meanwhile, however, it can be shown that there is a substantial basis of truth in all those affirmations concerning the nature of Christ which are contained in the Creeds. If some of the articles of the *Quicunque Vult* seem to us now to transcend the region of the scientifically ascertainable and to be excessively precise, if the religious sense in these days shrinks from that boldness of metaphysical speculation concerning the Divine Nature, which was considered by the makers of the Creeds and by the theologians of the past to be a pious and proper exercise of the understanding, if we now believe that the mischief arising from the compulsion of all Christians to assent to elaborately constructed dogmas is likely to be greater than that of allowing a larger liberty of belief to all, yet we cannot on reflection but acknowledge the present value, when they are rightly understood, of those expressions in the Apostles' and Nicene Creeds in which Jesus Christ is spoken of as the " Son of God," "begotten not made," " being of one substance with the Father," " by Whom all things were made." It may be, and indeed it unquestionably is the fact, that these expressions are cast in a mould furnished by the conceptions concerning the method of the Divine revelation, which were current in the earlier centuries of our era; it may be that a term which describes the method of human generation can only by a figure of speech represent the origination of that nature which was manifested to the world in the wisdom and transcendent lovableness and purity of Christ; it may be that the statement that Jesus Christ was the agent of the Invisible Power in making the world is a statement which, however true, in its literal signification is capable of no historical or scientific verification, and therefore cannot be brought into a parallel line with other articles of the Christian faith for which a substantial historical or scientific groundwork can be found; yet it would be difficult to frame other definitions which would serve better to express to the generality of men and women what is necessary to a right faith respecting the manifestation of the Supreme Power which is made in perfect human character as it is exhibited in Christ, respecting the Divine authorship of that higher nature in Christ of which His perfect character was the expression, and respecting the utter wisdom, benevolence, and mercifulness with which the operations of the Supreme Power have ever been carried on.

No doubt erroneous opinions have in the course of the centuries encrusted the popular belief concerning the manifestation of the Supreme Power in Jesus Christ and the mediatorial functions which Christ has fulfilled between God and man. For example, the idea of the sacrifice of an innocent victim to appease the outraged feelings of a heavenly Father angered by sin, is notably a survival from an age when a grossly ignorant conception was current concerning the nature of the deity. Still there is a profound truth underlying the popular doctrine of the Atonement, viz., that Christ in voluntarily devoting Himself to death to attest the truth of His teaching concerning God, and to attract men to give heed to it, acted in accordance with the general law, that it is only by self-sacrifice that men can convey substantial benefit to others. For the purposes of practical religion we cannot afford to lose sight of, or to obscure, that view of the efficacy of the death of Christ, which He Himself has set forth in the words, "I, if I be lifted up, shall draw all men unto Me;" nor can we in any way diminish the significance of Christ's mediatorial function in representing God to men, and giving to them the highest conception of the beauty and holiness of His character.

There is yet another way in which on reflection we are compelled to regard the "Infinite and Eternal Energy from which all things proceed." We are all consciously acted upon by inward impulses inclining us towards the love and pursuit of what is good and pure and true. When we do wrong we are inwardly reproved for it, when we do right we are inwardly commended. When two courses of action are open to us, and we are not certain which is right to take, we have only to reflect awhile in attention to the voice which speaks within us, and if the question be not too complex, our doubt is infallibly removed. Not only are we conscious of such experiences in ourselves, but we note them in others, and we find that they are shared in a greater or less degree by all our fellow-creatures. We have our own private predilections, tastes, prejudices, sympathies, and antipathies, which seem to belong to our very selves ; but these inward monitions of goodness are the same in others as in ourselves. When they are kept free from intermixture with impulses which arise from the different dispositions of different individuals, they are found to be identical in all men, so that they appear to stand, so to speak, altogether outside the region of self.

Now, on the supposition that "every phenomenon is a manifestation of some Power by which we are acted on," we are forced to hold that we ourselves, and all other men, are in the totality of our complex natures separately beings through whom a manifestation of the Supreme Power is made. We are each, as it has been well expressed,[*] delegated parts of God, endowed as men with certain peculiar powers, but yet presenting the same kind of manifestation of God as that which is afforded by other objects in the universe. But a quite distinct manifestation of God is made within us by those inward moral and spiritual monitions which are not peculiar to ourselves, but are shared by others, and are the same in them as in us. As to the way in which those monitions have come to operate within us it is foreign to our present argument to enquire. The only fact with which we have now to deal in connection with them is, that man, and especially civilized man as he is constituted at present, is acted upon by these monitions; and this being so, and God being the "Infinite and Eternal Energy, from which all things

[*] Martineau, *The Seat of Authority in Religion*, p. 35.

proceed," they cannot but be regarded as affording a separate kind of manifestation of God, a manifestation that is markedly distinct from that which is afforded by us as personal beings with each his own private individuality. It is impossible then to avoid arriving at the conclusion, that, as the Supreme Power of the universe is manifested in and through the phenomena of the material universe, in which we may include ourselves, as well as, in and through morally perfect humanity, so He is manifested in and through those moral and spiritual impulses which act more or less upon all men outside the region of their own personality.

This is the truth that has hitherto been witnessed to the world in the Christian doctrine of the Holy Spirit. In respect to this doctrine, again, it will be noted that mistakes have arisen from a too anthropomorphic view of the nature and actions of God, from a too literal interpretation of certain phrases of the New Testament, and from the excessive tendency to systematize and define, which have characterized the theology of the past. The teaching of the Christian Church concerning God the Holy Spirit has suffered perhaps more injury than the other branches of its doctrine concerning God from the adoption of the word " person " to express the different aspects of the Divine nature, corresponding to the different manifestations of God which were first denoted by the Greek word ὑπόστασις. It has been associated with limited conceptions as to the times and methods in which this manifestation has been made among men, it has tended to maintain an erroneous opinion of the nature of the composition of the sacred literature of Christianity, to the detriment of its authority at the present day, and it has seriously discredited in comparison those contributions to moral and religious truth which are furnished by the poet, the scientist, the artist, the historian, and especially by the student of religion who endeavours to give expression to the new thoughts of God which he believes he has acquired from the very source of truth itself.

Still, while noticing what may be called the popular abuse of the doctrine of the Christian Church concerning the Holy Spirit of God, and while recognizing that some of the articles of the Creed, in which it is expressed, appear now to trench too much upon ground that is beyond the possibility of accurate definition, yet, as in the case of the other articles of the Creed, it is needful for us to bear in mind that these each indicate an aspect of the manifestation of the Infinite Power, which it is important to keep in view, as for instance, that the new intimations of religious truth which are made known to the world by gifted men are not of their own origination, but of Divine suggestion, and that the Supreme Power is to be thought of and adored by men in reference to the influence He directly exerts upon their thoughts and feelings, as well as to the other manifestations of His power and energy,—truths which are enshrined in the statements that " He spake by the Prophets," and that " together with the Father and the Son He is worshipped and glorified."

By the process of reasoning we have thus far carried

on we are led to the recognition of a triple manifestation of God, in nature and the laws of nature, in perfect humanity, and in the higher impulses which act upon men. Whether there are other manifestations of God which may be distinguished from these, we cannot tell. Constituted as we are at present, our consciousness cannot transcend these limits, while any conception of God which falls short of them is necessarily imperfect and so far erroneous. The Christian Church has done invaluable service in popularizing this truth of the triple manifestation of God by means of its doctrine of the Trinity in Unity. No doubt, the terms in which the doctrine has been expressed have been inadequate and misleading to many, as those who first framed it foresaw.* The use of the word "person," which, as has been already remarked, by no means exactly represents the Greek ὑπόστασις, and which conveys to us now a meaning somewhat different even from that of the Latin word *persona*, has tended to maintain in the popular mind a tendency towards tritheism, or what has been styled, not without foundation, a belief in the Deity as a triad of "non-natural men." There may be reasons for regretting with Calvin that the word "Trinity," a non-biblical word, and a word that does not appear even in the Nicene Creed, should have been adopted into the Christian

---

* "When we deal with words that require some training to understand them, different people take them in senses not only different but absolutely opposed to each other."—Athanasius, *De Sententia Dionys.* 18.

doctrine of God; yet when we consider how inadequate are the resources of language for expressing Divine truth, it is difficult to see how in the past any more suitable words could have been chosen; though now, as we have had so much experience of the abuse of them, it is most necessary for it to be made known that they but very imperfectly express, as skilled theologians * allow, the mysterious verities, which human language at the best can only indicate and not define.

When we consider how repugnant to sound reason and common sense is the popular view of the Trinity in Unity even yet, when we remember in what an audaciously irrational way the relations between the Three Persons of the Godhead are still sometimes spoken of, and in what intricate verbal subtilties the popular preaching of the subject has tended uselessly to entangle the mind, it is not surprising that many thoughtful men should now be inclined towards Unitarianism rather than Trinitarianism as the more accurate doctrine concerning the nature of God. Still it should

---

* "It may be unmeaning not only to number the Supreme Being with other beings, but to subject Him to number in regard to His own intrinsic characteristics. That is, to apply arithmetical notions to Him may be as unphilosophical as it is profane. Though he is at once Father, Son, and Holy Ghost, the word " Trinity " belongs to those notions of Him which are forced on us by the necessity of our finite conceptions."—J. H. Newman, *Grammar of Assent*, 4th ed. p. 47.

"It was only with an expressed apology for the imperfection of human language that the Church spoke of the Divine Three, as *Three Persons* at all. But 'we have no celestial language,' and the word is the only one which will express what Christ's language implies about Himself, the Father, and the Spirit. Only while we use it, it must be understood to express mutual inclusion not mutual exclusion."—C. Gore, *Lux Mundi*, p.336.

be remembered that Unitarianism is just as much a dogmatic system as Trinitarianism is. Definition always implies the exclusion of something, and when we define the Divine nature as a Unity, we exclude the idea of its diversity—a much more serious dogmatic error than any that can result from the popular misapprehension of the doctrine of the Trinity in Unity. Already we see the effect of this error in the too exclusive attention which cultivated minds are giving to the manifestation of God which is presented in the phenomena of Nature, and the growing neglect of that witness to the mercifulness and lovableness of God which is derived from the contemplation of perfect humanity as it is exhibited in Jesus Christ, and from the best impulses that act upon individual men. If Trinitarianism as a dogmatic system is to be supplanted by a Unitarianism that shall be rigidly consistent with its title, then there will prevail among men an inferior conception of the character of the Infinite Power and a correspondingly inferior conception of the highest standard of human duty. Love will have a less substantial sanction among the virtues than justice, and men will be borne back to a pre-Christian system of morality, of which the dominant principle will be the promotion of the advancement of the type without regard to the claims of the individual. No, the doctrine concerning God which is to be the foundation of the morality of the future cannot be Unitarianism. In its conception of the Divine nature the world in the last eighteen centuries has not been going backward. The majority of Christians cannot have been nourishing themselves on a doctrine concerning God which is at the heart a lie.* However inadequate we may now find the verbal expression of that doctrine, it is impossible to believe that in its substance it is erroneous. It is from the ranks of those who have held it that have been produced the noblest characters with which this world has been blessed. And from the very fear lest that great succession of the saints should be interrupted we shall be wise not to part with the venerable symbols of the faith by which they lived, till we can find some more perfect way of expressing the truths which underlie them.

* "No thought that ever dwelt honestly as true in the heart of man but *was* an honest insight into God's truth on man's part, and *has* an essential truth in it which endures through all changes, an everlasting possession for us all."—Carlyle, *Heroes and Hero Worship*, Lecture IV.

CHAPTER III.

THE FUTURE LIFE.

ONE of the foremost of the problems with which religion is concerned, is that of the future state of the individual man. Christianity has progressed more by virtue of its doctrine of immortality than of any of its other doctrines. It has taught it positively as a revelation; but, as a revelation merely, it will not be accepted by those who have been trained in the modern school or reasoning. It particularly behoves us then to view the doctrine, as far as possible, in a strictly scientific light, so that it may be discovered whether there is or is not reasonable ground for believing it.

Now, the first thing to be noted in reference to this subject is, that the sciences which relate to man in his physical condition can tell us nothing positively as to his prospect of continuing to live after the decay of his body. It is a subject which lies outside their scope. They have to do with phenomena which are bounded by death, and the students of those sciences have no data for carrying their investigations further: they are in possession of no facts, which would authorize them to make any definite pronouncement for or against the future life of man. They may argue that when a man dies he appears to come to an end just as a beast or a plant, and therefore the probability is that like a beast or a plant he actually ceases to be. But neither the beast nor the plant perishes utterly. They are resolved at death into their constituent elements. In the case of the beasts especially, it is conceivable that the sentient life which they possessed is not destroyed, any more than the particles of matter in which they were embodied. Like those particles of matter it may undergo a transformation merely, though we cannot conceive of what sort it may be. Anyhow, it is impossible to prove that there is no life after death possible to the brutes. Similarly, it is impossible to prove that the life of man after death does not undergo transformation rather than destruction.

The probability that this is so is much stronger in the case of man than of the brute, for man is far more than a sentient animal with but imperfectly developed reasoning faculties: he is possessed of extraordinary volitional, emotional, intellectual, and moral powers: he is capable of unlimited ascension in the scale of moral character. Though subject to similar laws in the physical sphere with the brutes, he partakes of an entirely different order of experiences in the moral sphere, and has a moral growth or decay just as he has a physical growth or decay. Now, if in respect of the life which pertains to him physically, it is impossible to say of man that he perishes utterly at death, still less can that be affirmed of him in respect to that other kind of life which he seems to live in relation to the moral phenomena of which he is the subject. Nay, it may even be argued, that seeing that the law of the conversation of energy operates everywhere in Nature, it is impossible that the highest kind of energy of which we have any experience, viz., that which is exhibited in the developed emotional, volitional, intellectual, and especially moral life of man, can be the solitary exceptions to that law,—and that therefore it is utterly improbable that man is destructible by death.

However this may be, the one thing indisputable is, that physical and biological science can affirm or deny nothing with respect to the future life of man; and those who are most proficient in those sciences are quite ready to acknowledge this. Science, then, as the term is generally used, leaves the question open. Our ordinary method of arriving at positive knowledge fails us here. All we can learn by means of it is, that man may, or may not, continue to live after the dissolution of his body into its constituent elements.

But this is a question which, as regards its bearing on the religious thought and the moral conduct of each individual, cannot be treated as an open one. A man may apparently take up a perfectly reasonable position when he says, " I cannot tell whether or not there is a future state. I am necessarily an Agnostic on that subject, because there are no scientific data to go upon." But in the conduct of life he cannot help acting on one supposition or the other, and practically it will be found that to doubt the future life is to ignore it altogether in its relation to conduct. No man can build a solid structure on an uncertain foundation, and it is impossible for us to order our moral conduct according to ideals which can only have their justification and consummation in a life beyond the grave, if we have no positive opinion as to whether or not there is such a life at all. The consequence is, that the standard of morality that we necessarily keep in view, if we leave the question of the future life an open one in our minds, is a standard based on the negative of the question. At least we may be fairly certain about what is calculated to procure our well-being in this life, such as it is. The rewards and punishments attached to good and bad conduct here are fixed and determinate after their kind, and they afford a substantial basis for moral action of a certain sort. We know positively that such and such courses of action are judicious and politic in relation to our present mode of existence, and therefore, if we hold ourselves to be utterly ignorant of whether there is another life, we will shape our actions according to what we do know and with no reference to what we do not know. Yet in doing this we may make a great mistake. If there should happen to be a future life after all, it might prove eventually that in some important respects we had lived our earthly lives wrongly; so that it is in the highest degree injudicious to order our conduct entirely in accordance with the supposition that we perish utterly at death.

Moreover, it is not only injudicious thus to practically assume the negative of a profoundly important question, but it is in the highest degree unscientific to do so. There is hardly any fault greater from the scientific point of view than to decide without reflection in favour of one of two alternative opinions. Now, in this case, one opinion or the other must be true, and, therefore, it is a matter of grave importance as regards the right conduct of life that we should consider whether there may not be some other kind of evidence available on the subject, different from that which is supplied by the physical sciences. That there is such evidence will be shown later; but it will be worth while first to consider which of the two opinions as to man's prospect of life after the dissolution of the body it would be most advantageous to us to discover to be true, or, in the possible absence of sufficient evidence, to assume to be true, seeing that we must for practical purposes build on the supposition of the truth of one or the other.

Now, on this point there can be little doubt or controversy. Almost all those who are qualified to form a right judgment on the subject would say unhesitatingly, that it would be better for men, as regards their happiness as well as their moral conduct, to be able to look forward to another life as the continuation and completion of this than to repose in the opinion that they perish utterly when the breath leaves their bodies. Even granting that men can keep themselves pure, and live nobly laborious and self-sacrificing lives without having any hope of a future life, it is very doubtful whether they could rise to the full height of their various capabilities for good, unless they were sustained and stimulated by the thought of possible spheres of usefulness open to them hereafter. Self-culture for its own sake, apart from the effect it might have on one's own present condition and that of others, would, without such a prospect, fail of its highest encouragement. Moreover, it is only the purest minds and those most richly endowed by Nature who would be capable of strenuous and self-abnegating endeavour in the use of their powers. The vast majority could hardly be expected to rise above the ideal of getting as much enjoyment, and that chiefly of a sensual kind, out of this life as possible. Their motto would practically be, "Let us eat and drink, for to-morrow we die."

The effect on the happiness of the race of a general disbelief in a future life would be still more disastrous. To hold that our loved relations and friends who have gone from us, have departed into nothingness, to have no hope that all our highest and purest aspirations will eventually be satisfied, that all the wrong done in this world will eventually be righted, that all the untoward circumstances suffered without their fault by so many thousands of our fellow-creatures will be compensated to their good, that everyone will some time or other be exactly rewarded according to his works, and that infinite Mercy, as well as infinite Justice will hereafter be visited upon every living thing—to have no such hopes as these is to be deprived of that which is needed, not only to furnish the best incentives to our moral action, but to preserve us from the deadening belief that the Universe is but the sport of a malign chance, that human life is a prolonged deceit, and that consciousness is the saddest of all accidents in the evolution of sentient things.

> " My own dim life should teach me this,
> That life shall live for evermore,
> Else Earth is darkness at the core,
> And dust and ashes all that is." *

It is impossible to resist this conclusion. The only logical attitude of man towards the present constitution of things, when the possibility of a future life is negatived, is pessimism. And pessimism, whether it be true or false, is the saddest and darkest philosophy of life that anyone can feel constrained to adopt.

On the other hand, it is a fact which none will care to dispute, that the gain to human happiness as well as human goodness, from a belief in a future life has been immense. How else could the world have been afforded so many examples of men and women afflicted with dire infirmities and oppressed with many poignant cares, who were yet in a constant condition of humble contentment and cheerfulness? How else could we have heard of so many persons endowed with the same evil passions as others, and with the same natural desires for self-gratification and self-glory, renouncing all thought of earthly pleasure, and living what may well be called crucified lives on behalf of their fellow-

* Tennyson, *In Memoriam*.

creatures? How else could the lofty graces of love, and courtesy, and reverence, and self-denial have blossomed so nobly in so many lowly hearts? It cannot be denied that by far the highest attainments in conduct and disposition from the dawn of history to the present hour are to be associated with a vivid belief in the continuance of man's life beyond the grave. It is not a little significant that hitherto the purest moral teaching even in non-Christian quarters has always been enunciated by those who have been believers in God and a future life; while such lives of unapproached sanctity as have been nourished in the Christian Church have been lived only by men who, without meriting the epithet of other-worldly, have regarded the things of the life to come as the most substantial, nay, the only realities.

It seems, then, as though there were an inseparable connection between the belief in immortality and the possibility of well-being and goodness of the highest kind, so that, when we compare the two opinions as to man's prospects in the future in regard to their effect on human happiness and conduct, there is no doubt as to which it would be wise to prefer, if the probability in favour of each were otherwise equal, and we were forced in the absence of a preponderance of evidence on either side, to choose between the two.

But it cannot truly be said that the probabilities in favour of each opinion are equal. It is difficult to think that a belief that has hitherto been so widely spread, that indeed has been almost universal among the highest races, and that has had such an excellent moral effect upon the world can have been wholly false. Mr. Herbert Spencer has laid great stress on the witness to the substantial truth of a belief which is afforded by the fact of its having been universally held; and upon that argument in part he has founded his doctrine of the Inscrutable Power manifested behind phenomena. The same argument may be applied as exactly to the doctrine of a future life. It may be that that belief had an ignoble beginning, just as had the developed belief in God. Yet Mr. Herbert Spencer has shewn how at the outset there was a germ of truth contained in the primitive conception of God, and by precisely similar reasoning it can be shown that there may have been originally a germ of truth in the crude belief of our ancestors respecting the continued existence of their departed friends.

But whatever weight may be attached to the argument from the universality of the belief in a future life, there can be little question as to the reasonableness which it gains from the fact of its having been held by the wisest and best men whom the world has seen. It is noteworthy that not a single poet who has a true title to be called great has ever been a disbeliever in immortality. Without going back to distant times and mentioning such names as those of Homer and the Greek dramatists, and Dante, or even Shakspeare and Milton, who all lived in days when the belief was scarcely called in question, it is sufficient to refer to Tennyson and Browning in England, Victor Hugo in France, and

Goethe in Germany, as men of profoundly original thought who have keenly felt the new intellectual influences of our own time, and have yet not simply retained their belief in a future life as a pious opinion in which they were brought up, but have proclaimed it as an important particular of the truth which they have discerned for themselves and have felt constrained to publish to the world. Indeed, hardly a single instance can be quoted of any man of remarkable genius in any age who has doubted that there was a higher destiny in store for the human race than any that can possibly be fulfilled on earth. Even in a state of society which was pervaded by a rapidly spreading scepticism, Cicero, not the most admirable in every respect of the great men of his time, yet deserving nevertheless of the epithet conferred upon him by Byron of "Rome's least mortal mind," could say,—"Somehow or other there clings to one's mind an assurance of a life to come, else who would be so foolish as to cleave to this life with its manifold toils and perils?"

Now men like these, especially the poets whose names have been mentioned, cannot be said to carry no greater weight with them than others, when they speak on this momentous though deeply mysterious subject. We concede to the poets a power, exceeding that possessed by other men, of discovering and telling forth what is true in relation to human life and the deeper problems of Nature. A man becomes really great as a poet in proportion to the way in which he brings to light truths that are hidden from common men; and his greatness is still further demonstrated in the course of years when it is found that the truths he enunciated were truths not only in relation to the circumstances of his own country and his own time, but truths for every country and for all time. In whatever way the greater poets arrive at such truths, and none has yet succeeded in tracking the courses of thought in a poet's mind, we cannot but discern and acknowledge that they have some extraordinary means of access to the very sources of truth, and, therefore, whenever they pronounce themselves positively even on subjects about which by ordinary processes of reasoning there is no possibility of our arriving at certain knowledge, they are entitled to be listened to with respectful and even docile attention.

Still more may this be claimed for those who are gifted with an extraordinary power of discovering what is true in relation to conduct and morals. There is nothing nearly so wonderful in the history of human thought as the production of the ethical system of Christianity. That system not only stands before any other system of morals that has yet been enunciated, but the wisdom of its Founder in respect to His power of discerning moral truth is acknowledged by all competent authorities to be unerring. No single flaw in His moral teaching or in His life has ever yet been demonstrated, and none of the wisest and purest-minded of those who have lived since His time have ever dreamt of improving upon it. It is a system of morals so perfect indeed that it has been thought too high for common men; yet that only helps to prove the unrivalled power which Christ exhibited in providing principles of conduct which should suffice for the very highest intellectual and moral capacities in the most advanced stage of development of the race. Now, one of the essential principles of Christ's teaching was, that what we call death makes no interruption to the life of man. He did not even use the word death in the signification in which we use it, but spoke of those who had departed this life, as though they were merely asleep. The only time He ever argued on the subject was when He was pressed by the Sadducees with a quibbling question respecting the resurrection. He then, speaking of the patriarchs who had been dead hundreds of years before, used the expression that they were still "living unto God," for "all live unto Him." That is, to the Supreme Power of the universe there is no such thing as the death of man in the sense in which we speak of it. He takes no cognizance of the change that is deemed so all-important by us. On other occasions Christ treated the fact of man's continuance of life after the dissolution of his body as so natural and patent that He never argued in favour of it, but spoke of it as a self-evident truth, or declared it in language similar to that which He used when He enunciated moral truth. In fact, His teaching concerning the future life was bound up indissolubly with His teaching concerning the right principles of conduct. None can live that highest kind of life, the principles of which are set forth in the Sermon on the Mount, except he hold the doctrine which is associated with it. And as a matter of fact, as has already been remarked, those who have reached the highest attainment in character through the power with which Christianity has furnished them, are those who have most nearly shared Christ's view of the sleep-like character of death.

Now the argument which applies to the value of the testimony concerning immortality which is given by the poets applies with double force to the kind of testimony given by Christ. If we cannot trace exactly the process by which the great poets arrive at the truths which they utter, and which lapse of time only tends to confirm, still less can we conceive exactly by what means such an unerring knowledge of moral truth was acquired by the young Jew, who, living a life of simple labour in a now remote age, uttered treasures of wisdom which the highest and purest minds, quickened by the accumulated intellectual resources of many centuries, are not able fully to fathom and comprehend, let alone to appraise at their full value. That He was able in some way in which other men have not been able to get at the very sources of truth, those persons will be among the readiest to acknowledge who are averse to any superhuman theory of Christ's origin and nature. They cannot, any more than others, deny that He "spake as never man spake" concerning moral truth, and acknowledging this, and noticing also that He spake with the same confidence concerning man's existence hereafter, and that His teaching on the two subjects was of one piece, they cannot well avoid arriving at the conclusion, that moral truth and the truth concerning the future destiny of man are in some way or another connected, and that He Who spake with an authority that cannot but be admitted on the one subject, must be allowed to speak with equal authority on the other.

This is what devout Christians in all ages have believed. They have found Jesus worthy of implicit trust when He told them how to regulate their lives, and they have judged Him therefore worthy to be believed when He spoke to them also of the "life eternal." In accepting His word on both these subjects and in acting according to it, they have found literally "a peace which the world cannot give." They have aspired and endeavoured to "do the will of God," as He declared it; and "through the hope set before them" they have found the necessary power to do it, and so there has to come to them the blessed assurance that they were not only doing but believing what was true. Not the least part of the satisfaction which the disciples of Christ have derived from accepting all His teaching in its fulness is, that they have felt an internal witness of its truth in both particulars. They have been impelled towards the ethical teaching of Christ by those pure monitions felt within them, yet distinguishable from their own personal and selfish inclinations, which they were accustomed to think of, and, as we have seen, rightly, as a distinct manifestation within them of the Supreme Power; they have found that they were impelled by the same monitions towards the acceptance of Christ's teaching concerning the life to come, for they have felt themselves urged as a duty to attribute good motives and intentions to God, just as to one another; and perceiving that it was impossible to think of Him as good, if He allowed death to be the utter annihilation of the existence of good men and to be the utter termination of all pure human love and lofty human aspiration, they have deemed themselves inwardly moved by God Himself to believe Christ's doctrine of the future life. That doctrine had thus its confirmation from the voice of God within them, and so it appeared not only that it was true, but that it came in the first instance from the fount of truth—from God Himself, and that Christ in giving utterance to it was, as He said, but the mouthpiece of God.

This apparent Divine origin of the doctrine of the future life has been always regarded by Christians as the most important evidence of its truth. They have supposed it to have been learnt by direct communication from God by the method which has been already referred to as that of revelation. Now Jesus stands alone among all those who have been the instruments for communicating moral and religious truth to others, in this respect, that His knowledge on this subject was, so far as men have been able to discover since, as unerring as it was profound. Hence it was held that He spoke the very mind of God, and thus must have been related to God in a peculiar way in which ordinary men are not—the relationship being defined in the later dogmas of the Church. We have already referred to the question as to whether or not those dogmas are entitled to be regarded as giving an infallibly accurate description of the nature of Christ and of God. However this may be, there can be no doubt that a peculiar and an unprecedented authority attaches to the pronouncements of Jesus on moral and religious truth,—so much so that His mere word in favour of any doctrine is of the nature of positive proof of it, and we are justified in accepting with implicit trust in their truth even such statements of His as pass our powers of comprehension.

It cannot be said then that we have absolutely no evidence in favour of the future life. On the contrary there is evidence, which to those who weigh it rightly has very substantial value. True, it is not exactly evidence of a kind that amounts to a positive demonstration. It cannot make any and all men certain of the future life, in a way in which they can be made certain of a historical fact or of a truth of mathematics. Still it is deserving of the name of scientific evidence nevertheless, for it is based on facts and phenomena which are capable of scientific analysis, and it can make the future life at least in a very high degree probable, so as, coupled with other considerations, to reasonably incline us to treat it as a certainty.

This then is what it appears wise for us to do. When we reflect that for the conduct of life we are unable to leave the question of the future life an open one, but are compelled to choose between the one alternative and the other; when we take note of the fact that the highest happiness and the greatest possibility of the goodness of the race are bound up with the belief of the future life; and when we remember further that that belief has not only been held by the wisest and best of men, but has been suggested to them by what they have had reason to regard as the very Spirit of God within them; then, on the triple ground of reason, duty, and expediency, it seems right that we should reject utterly the thought of our extinction at death, and determine once for all to live our lives as those who have an infinite future before them.

In making this resolution to treat the probability of the future life as a certainty, we need by no means pledge ourselves to accept the opinions concerning the future state which have been, or are, popularly held; nor need we bind ourselves to shape our conceptions of what will take place hereafter by the literal phraseology of the Bible. It is only too probable that any definite speculation concerning the conditions of man's life in another state of being will be wide of the mark, as we have no faculties for accurately figuring to ourselves things of which we have absolutely no experience. We may dismiss from our minds therefore any obligation to conform our ideas of what will take place hereafter to the doctrine of endless material punishment for all who have departed this life without being believers in Christ, as held by the Evangelical Protestant, or to the doctrine of purgatory as held by the Roman Catholic. One thing is absolutely certain, that any kind of speculation concerning the future state is fundamentally wrong, in which it is implied that things will happen to men which are plainly not in accordance with infinite Justice and Love. If, moreover, it be urged that material things are spoken of in the descriptions of the Judgment and of Heaven and Hell in the New Testament, it must be explained that expressions of this sort can only rightly serve to denote the fact, that there will be a visitation upon men in the next life of the consequences of their actions in this, and that the good will be recompensed and the bad punished according to their works. *How* this will be done we cannot conceive, and need not know; it is sufficient that we convince ourselves that it *will* be done.

More than this none can tell us, not even Christ. He Himself acknowledged His ignorance of the circumstances of the Judgment, notably of the time of it.* Prophecy, the utterance of what it is the design of the Supreme Power to effect in the future, does not and cannot deal with details. Whenever the attempt has been made by prophecy, or by others on behalf of prophecy, it has signally failed. It is only moral and religious knowledge, not natural and historical, that is communicated to us through the agency of the Divine Spirit, and the intimation of the future life that Jesus was the means of communicating to men, and that is confirmed by a testimony within us, is entirely of that character. It assures us that there *is* a future in store for men beyond physical death, because the vindication of the Divine Justice and Benevolence requires it. More than that it does not tell us, and it is amply

* St. Mark xiii. 32.

sufficient for the sustentation of our hopes and the regulation of our conduct. It is true that numerous intricate problems suggest themselves to our minds when the thought of our future existence is before us; but long centuries of idle and useless speculation on the subject ought at least to have taught us the vanity of attempting to solve such problems; and that deeper sense of reverence towards the Inscrutable Power which science is imparting to us ought to make us see the propriety of not indulging an audacious curiosity which cannot be satisfied, and of rather contenting ourselves with the assurance that everything will happen hereafter in accordance with the dictates of a wisdom, in comparison with which the highest imaginations of man are but folly. We need not then attempt to form the slightest definite conception as to what our future existence will be like, except that it will be personal and self-conscious, as of that there seems the very strongest moral probability.*

* " Without thought, without love, without reverence, without will, without objects (and none but personal beings can have these), what remains to fill the phrase 'highest life'? (quoting Schleiermacher). Psychologically, there can be no greater descent than the steps from the personal to the impersonal."—Martineau, *A Study of Religion*, Vol. II., p. 368.

"That each who seems a separate whole,
    Should move his rounds, and fusing all
    The skirts of self again, should fall
Re-merging in the general soul,

Is faith as vague as all unsweet:
    Eternal form shall still divide
    The eternal soul from all beside;
And I shall know him when we meet."
                    Tennyson, *In Memoriam*, XLVII.

If we do but school ourselves to believe that we and the whole race will still continue to be dealt with in a manner that is divinely paternal, we shall be acting in a much more becoming way, and in a way that will bring far more satisfaction to ourselves, than if we follow in the speculative footsteps of the past.

Our hope of the future, if it is thus framed, may be vague, but it will wholly suffice for the moral purpose which it is its function to serve. Even a vague hope may serve to entirely uplift a man and induce him to achieve the best he is capable of. There is a profound perception of this truth manifested in the description given by Æschylus of the way in which Prometheus, or Forethought, roused the dejected spirit of primitive man to achieve his destiny on earth—

  ΠΡ. θνητούς γ' ἔπαυσα μὴ προδέρκεσθαι μόρον.
  ΧΟ. τὸ ποῖον εὑρὼν τῆσδε φάρμακον νόσου;
  ΠΡ. τυφλὰς ἐν αὐτοῖς ἐλπίδας κατῴκισα.

"Blind" hopes of the possibilities that lay before them as the end of their toil and self-discipline were sufficient to rouse men to the activity which enabled them at first to fulfil their part of replenishing the earth and subduing it; "blind" hopes of what he may in time effect furnish the stimulus which incites the young man to brace up his energies and prepare himself by strenuous labour for the earnest struggle of his maturer years; and "blind" hopes of gain to be won for science and good to be achieved for the race have hitherto proved all-sufficient to sustain the scientist and the philanthropist in the arduous and prolonged tasks which they have voluntarily undertaken. Let us but set before ourselves " blind," through real and substantial, hopes of a future which awaits us in the state of existence upon which we shall enter at death, and we shall find that they are amply sufficient to cheer and gladden us throughout the vicissitudes of this life of much toil and sorrow, to keep us ever in a state of contented trust that all is right in the constitution of the universe, and to spur us on so to use all our gifts, whether religious, moral, intellectual, or physical in the service of the Infinite Power and in accordance with His eternal laws, that as we increase in age and experience we shall increase in manifold capacity for good, and in fitness for a higher and happier sphere of activity in the ages to come.

CHAPTER IV.

MIRACLES.

THE two beliefs for which a scientific basis has been found in the two preceding chapters are quite sufficient in themselves to be the groundwork and mainstay of our personal religion. Indeed, when we analyse the motives and hopes which inspire our noblest thought and action, and nerve and comfort us best in trial, we find that they are all wrapt up in the belief in God and in a future life. Still there are other matters of religious interest about which we are naturally anxious to have, if possible, clear ideas, although they cannot be regarded as of equal importance with those already discussed. In particular, the subject of miracles is one which presses seriously now on the thought of those who are desirous of knowing what ought to be believed respecting the records of the life of Christ and the early history of the Church.

It is plain that important issues depend on the accuracy or otherwise of the representation of Jesus Christ which is given in the New Testament; yet the significance of the miracles attributed to Christ can by no means be regarded now in the same light as that in which it was till recently set forth by the apologists of the Christian religion. It can no longer be believed that "miracles are necessary to attest the truth of a revelation" in the sense in which that proposition has hitherto been maintained. We do not feel that we have a right to expect that, when anyone tells us anything fresh about religion or morals, he should enforce the credibility of his statements by performing some marvels in the material sphere. Moral truth and religious truth are to be proved, just as truth of physical science is to be proved, by observation and experiment and, when necessary, by correct logical argument. A new "revelation" is like a new scientific theory. A man promulgates a new doctrine in morals or theology, just as an observer of facts in nature promulgates a new doctrine concerning the correlation of those facts. We do not expect the scientist to prove his theory by working miracles, neither should we expect the prophet. It is by a strange oversight of the caution repeatedly given on the subject by Jesus Himself, that defenders of His religion have so unduly pressed the evidential value of His miracles. Without by any means conveying that His miracles had no significance, He repeatedly shrank, so we are told, from performing them as mere "signs." He openly condemned the state of mind of those who would not believe "except they saw signs and wonders,"[*] and indeed He went so far as to say, "An evil and adulterous generation seeketh after a sign."[†]

The mischief resulting from this kind of defence of

[*] St. John iv. 48.   [†] St. Matthew xii. 39.

Christianity is evidenced by the scepticism concerning moral and religious truth which it has produced. Very many persons, having been led to believe that " miracles are the proper proof of a revelation," and that, therefore, the truth of Christianity is inextricably bound up with the authenticity of the miracles attributed to Christ, when they have seen reason to doubt those miracles or some of them, have doubted also the truth of the religious and moral teaching of Christ.

As a matter of fact, there is no such connection between the miracles attributed to Christ and His teaching. The reports of the miracles of Christ might be in many particulars erroneous, and yet the ethical and religious statements of the Gospels be absolutely sound. These latter are proved by a different kind of evidence from the former, by the knowledge that is gained from a study of the different manifestations of religion in every quarter and every age, by the assent which they have received from the best and wisest of men, by the way in which, when they have been acted upon, they have transformed the lives of sinners, and by the testimony to their goodness and truth which we feel within ourselves.

It is quite possible that the Evangelists may have given a transcript of a religious and ethical teaching which is fundamentally true, though the representation they have given of the life of Jesus we may judge to be in some particulars improbable. Certainly a belief in the soundness of the moral and religious teaching attributed to Christ does not by any means involve a belief in the literal accuracy of all that is related about Him. A man may truly be said to be a believer in Christianity who is nevertheless in doubt about certain of the recorded miracles, or indeed all of them ; and even if he is wrong in doubting the miracles, his error cannot be said to be a moral and religious one. It is a moral and religious thing to believe in the moral and religious teaching of Christ, but it is not necessarily a moral and religious thing to believe in the miracles attributed to Christ. On the contrary, a man may be led to doubt the miracles from what is from his point of view actually a moral and religious motive, because when he honestly investigates them they seem to him to be untrue, and because he feels that he cannot and should not believe what is untrue.

The question of the authenticity of the miracles attributed to Christ must then be dissociated from the question of the truth of His religion. Still it is a question which has an importance of its own, and that not a small one, in regard to the light which the right answer to it throws on the nature of the personality of Christ. On that ground the Gospel miracles demand our most careful investigation, and it much behoves us to endeavour to ascertain whether or not they are true, or, if not all, at any rate which of them are true.

On the threshold of such an enquiry, however, we are met with an obstacle that seems entirely to bar our progress, viz., the total denial of the possibility of the miraculous. "Miracles do not happen," we are told very positively by some who profess to speak in the name of modern culture.* It is an assertion which has obtained a wide publicity, and has been accepted implicitly by a large number of persons. On the strength of it the life of Christ has been re-written by various writers, who have, each after his own peculiar fashion, eliminated from it the miraculous element, and have given to the world representations of the nature of Christ markedly different from that which is given in the Gospels.

Now such a proposition, notwithstanding the apparent weight of authority with which it is uttered, requires a great deal of enforcement before it can command the full assent even of those who have been trained to think in the most modern style. *Primâ facie* it is calculated to excite suspicion and opposition from its very positive and dogmatic form. If there is any one thing that we have had more forcibly impressed upon us than any other by the progress of science in the present century it is the need of caution in affirmation. The scientific spirit is essentially a spirit of dogmatic reserve; and it may be doubted whether any person of acknowledged authority in the scientific world of to-day would care to risk his reputation by stating outright that miracles do not happen, using the the word to cover all the occurrences narrated in the Bible which are commonly spoken of as miraculous. He might hold a very strong private opinion about the credibility of any accounts of miraculous occurrences

---

*The author of the phrase is Matthew Arnold, *Literature and Dogma*, Ed. 1883, Preface.

that have yet reached us, but he would probably hesitate long before he would say that miracles could not happen, have never happened, or even do not happen now.

But besides being unscientific in form, there is a certain vagueness of meaning about this proposition. Though in the present tense, it does not appear at first sight whether it relates to the past and the future as well as to the present. The phrase "miracles do not happen" may easily be read to mean that they could not happen and have never happened. We shall, however, deal more fairly with the author of it if we take it in an exactly literal sense. Then the argument will be, "We never hear of authentic miracles now, therefore there never have been any, and therefore the so-called miracles of the New Testament could not have happened." The argument is a plausible one, but it cannot be convincing till two objections to it have been met. The first is suggested by the familiar Protestant doctrine, that the period in which Christ appeared was a period favourable for the production of miracles, but that shortly after His disappearance those favourable conditions ceased, or for an express purpose were removed. Whatever historical and critical ground there may be for this doctrine, it is at least logically consequent. If the commencement of the Christian era was marked by a new phrase of spiritual development, it is not irrational to suppose that that period may have witnessed extraordinary physical occurrences accompanying the spiritual. It is a fact of considerable significance also that the extraordinary production of religious truth by the method previously discussed under the name of revelation has hitherto taken place for the most part in the East, and it is those particularly who are mentioned as the recipients of fresh revelations that are represented as being possessed of miraculous powers.

The person, then, who maintains that, because miracles do not happen now, therefore they have never happened at all, puts himself under the obligation of proving, that the conditions under which miracles are said to have been wrought in the East more than eighteen hundred years ago by men of exceptional spiritual endowment are exactly paralleled in Europe at the present day.

The other current doctrine about miracles suggests the second objection to the denial of the miracles of the New Testament. The Romanist argues that we have no ground for saying that miracles happened in the Christian Church up to a certain indefinite date, and after that date ceased. Instead, therefore, of waiting to controvert the conclusion of those who deny the miracles of the New Testament, he boldly challenges the premiss, that miracles do not happen now. He says that, on the contrary, miracles do happen, and have happened from the days when the New Testament was completed down to our own time. Is he right or wrong in saying this? He is wrong surely in so far as he accepts the so-called ecclesiastical miracles without discrimination, and is ready to assert a supernatural cause for occurrences which are plainly contrived by ordinary means in order to impress the vulgar, or which are natural events invested with a supernatural character by honest though uncritical historians. A glance at some of the miraculous stories of the Middle Ages may well serve to cast suspicion on any and all of the miracles of which the Romanist maintains there has been a continuous succession down to the present day. And yet it is impossible to study these and similar stories in a candid and judicial spirit, without being persuaded that there is a substantial residuum of fact in some of them, and that they afford, for example, instances of cures which have been effected by methods of which we have no ordinary experience. Making all deductions for uncritical or even unfaithful narrative, there can be little doubt but that in the alleged miracles of modern times we are brought face to face with very remarkable phenomena, only explicable on the supposition that they are due to exceptional action of mind over body, or, in the case of an interchange of influence, of mind over mind.

This is rendered all the more probable, because recent experiments in connection with hypnotism and telepathy have been attended with results, which appear to prove conclusively that certain diseases may be cured by other than ordinary medical means; and there is much likelihood, that in the not distant future a more exact and comprehensive study of certain psychological facts will furnish us with some remarkable discoveries concerning the possibilities of personal influence of a kind of which we have as yet little definite knowledge.

These are considerations which should make us strongly disinclined to assent to the proposition that "miracles" never occur now; and whatever weight we attach to them, they place an insurmountable difficulty in the way of our making a clean sweep of all the so-called miracles in the New Testament. Even though some of those miracles seem incapable of being classed with any modern case of healing of the kind that has just been alluded to, and are vastly more difficult to imagine as real occurrences, yet while we do find among the recorded works of Christ some cures of sickness, which are apparently similar to what we have heard of in recent years, we are absolutely unable to deny the possibility of the miraculous in the life of Christ. More than that, a careful investigation of different so-called miracles of this class may not only serve to convince us of their truth, but may logically incline us towards a belief in the possibility of some of the more difficult ones.

Now, when we analyse the miracles interspersed throughout the Gospels, we find that they are capable of being arranged in four or five different classes. There are, first, the miracles related in connection with the birth and infancy of Jesus, miracles in which He is not represented as having a personal agency. Such are the angelic messages, the conception by the Holy Ghost, the Star in the East, etc. Against these it is urged that similar miraculous stories are related in connection with other remarkable births, and they are therefore put down as legends which the pious imagination of the early Christians wove round the story of the Saviour's infancy. We may set this class of miracles aside for the present. Without conceding their falsehood, it must be maintained that the demonstration of their falsehood would not in the slightest degree affect the authenticity of others. It is necessary to insist upon this at the outset, for some people seem incapable of dissociating the miraculous stories related about Christ from those in which He is represented as the direct agent. In reality they are quite distinct, and depend for their verification upon evidence of a different character. Instead of rejecting these at once, and from their manifest spuriousness deducing the impossibility of all the other miracles, the proper plan surely is, to examine first those miracles which are ascribed to the action of Christ Himself, and then to proceed to investigate the evidence, documentary and other, which can be adduced in favour of the marvels which are said to have taken place at His birth. The result of the first investigation will have a very practical influence on the manner in which we shall be disposed to approach the second.

The next class of Gospel miracles that may be named is that which comprises occurrences, that might or might not be correctly explained, as natural events described in a supernatural way or with supernatural accessories. Among these we may include parts of the story of the Temptation, such as, " The devil taketh Him up into the Holy city, and setteth Him on a pinnacle of the Temple," in which it has been suggested that we may find traces of a supernatural colouring given to an actual struggle fought out by Jesus in solitude. The descent of the Holy Dove upon Christ at His Baptism may also be, as some old commentators have thought, a miraculous description of some natural circumstance that coincided with Christ's "going up out of the water." We have no data for disproving such explanations of various occurrences described in the Bible as miraculous, and it is not a matter of importance that they should be disproved, except we would maintain what it is needless and indeed impossible to maintain, that the writers of the Gospels were supernaturally preserved from every possible form of error, whether critical or historical, in their narratives. The most implicit faith in the genuineness and honesty of the Evangelists is quite compatible with the opinion, that they may have sometimes given a supernatural character to occurrences which, had they happened in our day, would have been differently described.

A very striking instance of how such a mistake might have been made by an Evangelist is furnished in the fifth chapter of St. John's Gospel. A description is there given of a famous medicinal pool called Bethesda. This pool has been identified on very good grounds with an intermittent spring now called the *Fountain of the Virgin*, which bubbles up at irregular intervals sometimes two or three times a day, and sometimes in summer once in two or three days. When these disturbances of the water mentioned in the Gospel took place, the medicinal properties of the pool were at their highest, and though there is nothing in the narrative to warrant the supposition that any person who bathed in the water was at once, as it were, miraculously cured, there is no doubt that the repeated use of such an intermittent and gaseous spring, as modern experience testifies, was likely to produce most beneficial results. In the then state of scientific knowledge the nature of medicinal springs was not understood, and it is not surprising therefore that such effects as those produced at the pool of Bethesda should have been attributed to supernatural agency. Accordingly the Jews conceived that an Angel went down at a certain season into the pool, and troubled the water. It was a pious and beautiful imagination, although manifestly to us it involves the error of assigning to a more remote and mysterious cause what is easily explained by a nearer and simpler one. The legend is recorded in the fourth verse of John v. in the Authorised Version, but has been expunged by the Revisers, as the verse is wanting in the majority of the best MSS., and contains internal evidences of its spuriousness. There is no doubt, however, that it was incorporated into other texts of the Gospel at a very early date. Now, it may be argued that the acknowledged spuriousness of the verse tends to acquit the the author of this Gospel of the liability to such an error as it exemplifies, but on the other hand the fact that a story so manifestly legendary was thus early embodied in the text of the New Testament by those who lived nearest to the Evangelists and most reverentially preserved their works, is strong evidence of the habit of thought with regard to the miraculous that prevailed in the earliest days of Christianity. It is only likely then that those who put together the first records of the life of Christ should have shared this habit of thought. We have no authority for affirming that, unlike all their contemporaries, they were possessed of such critical powers as we have but lately acquired from our accumulated knowledge of historical and scientific facts; and it is but reasonable to suppose, that certain occurrences recorded in the New Testament as having been brought about by supernatural agency, may have happened in strict accordance with natural law.

When, however, we apply ourselves to a careful investigation of another class of miracles, those immediately ascribed to the agency of Christ Himself, we cannot suppose the same reason for questioning the literal accuracy of the Gospel narratives. We simply cannot satisfactorily conceive of such occurrences as happening at all except in the way they are described. There is nothing in our ordinary experience which gives us the slightest clue as to how they could have taken place otherwise. If we do not accept the explanation given of them in the Gospels, we are forced to account for their appearance in their narrative by one of two expedients, which to the unprejudiced mind involve infinitely greater difficulties than that of accepting them for what they are stated to be. Either they were "thaumaturgic frauds" practised by Christ in order to impose upon the common people, "a concession," as Renan has put it, "forced from him by a passing necessity," or else they are mere inventions of the sacred writers. The first supposition, to those who have studied the character of Christ reverently and sympathetically, is absolutely untenable. Some *may* think He could have stooped to a long continued course of imposition, but those who have tried for long to *know* Christ are wholly convinced that He could not have done such a thing; and, whatever perplexity the miraculous may suggest to them, it would be infinitely easier to them to believe that He actually wrought miracles than that He only pretended to do so.

But the miracles ascribed to Christ may be inventions of the early Christians. It was in exact accordance with the taste and fashion of the age, that those who applied themselves to relate the story of One for whom they laid claims to divine origin should weave into that story a whole cycle of miracles. This is Strauss's assertion, and he has framed a theory to fit in with it. His theory is, that the earliest Jewish Christians came to believe in Jesus as the Messiah, that they had been brought up from childhood in the belief that the Messiah was to have certain distinguishing marks, that then stories circulated among them purporting to show how Jesus actually did all that, according to their notions, He ought to have done, and that these stories, being in perfect accordance with their preconceived notions, when once started were readily believed in, and in simple faith passed on from one to another, until in process of time they came to be recorded in the Gospels.

Now even if this theory were thought to be in some respects probable, if it were felt that there was a likelihood that the Jewish Christians might be inclined to attribute to Jesus some things which they had been brought up to believe as characteristic of the Messiah, in no way would this opinion satisfactorily account for the miracles purporting to be wrought by His personal agency. To imagine that all these stories are mere fabrications, gradually pieced together after our Lord's disappearance, is to endow the first Christians with gifts of invention which far transcend any powers of the human mind which have ever been exhibited before or since. For perfection of form, for dramatic accuracy, and for beauty of parabolic teaching, there would be nothing at all approaching them in the literature of fiction. We must put those untutored fishermen, slaves, artisans, and tradesmen, far above our Homers and Shakespeares, and acknowledge that in the narratives attributed to the Evangelists we possess the loftiest achievements of the imagination which have ever been attained. This of course is absurd. It is quite unthinkable that all the stories of the miracles of Christ, being such as they are, could have originated in the brains of those who wrote them down. The argument that other cycles of miracles in other remarkable lives had their origin in this way simply does not fit the case at all. The two kinds of narratives cannot be even compared together. When we read the Gospel according to St. Matthew, say, after Bede's Ecclesiastical History, not to mention the apocryphal lives of Christ, we recognize the difference at once. However much we may be inclined to suspect the accuracy of a narrative which deals in miracle, whatever natural repugnance we may feel to the acceptance of the possibility of the miraculous, the fabrication theory of all the miracles attributed to Christ is infinitely more unthinkable than that those miracles actually happened.

The best way surely to form an opinion as to their truth or falsehood is to approach the study of the text of the Gospels with a mind as free as possible from a bias either way. In a literary question so controverted internal evidence is of great value, and even if we cannot wholly rid ourselves of a prejudice against the miraculous, it is at least only fair that we should examine some of these stories related about Christ to see whether it may not be likely after all that they carry their own explanation with them. Not to go further afield let us take the incident narrated directly after the mention of the pool of Bethesda in St. John v. The Authorised Version afforded us an instance of a natural occurrence explained supernaturally—a fabricated miracle. In the following verses there is related what purports to be the cure by Jesus of the paralytic, who was unable to get himself conveyed to the pool when the water was "troubled." "When Jesus saw him lying, and knew that he had been now a long time in that case, He saith unto him, Wouldest thou be made whole? The sick man answered Him, Sir, I have no man, when the water is troubled, to put me into the pool: but while I am coming, another steppeth down before me. Jesus saith unto him, Arise, take up thy bed, and walk. And straightway the man was made whole, and took up his bed and walked."* Now is this miracle explicable by any of the theories we have been considering? Was it an imposition practised by Christ on the paralytic and the bystanders? Did He pretend to heal the man and satisfy both him and the others that he was healed? Was it a conjuring trick by which He made this helpless cripple appear to take up his bed and walk? That surely is quite out of the question. Well then is it a fabricated incident? Did no such thing happen at all? Was there no paralytic at the pool of Bethesda, and did Christ exercise no influence over such a man? There may be those who can fancy this; but on grounds of pure literary criticism there is no better reason for cutting out this part of the fifth chapter of St. John than there is for getting rid of the rest of the book. It may be left to the common sense of any ordinary reader to determine whether we have any justification for saying that something of the sort described by the Evangelist did not actually take place. There remains then only the supposition that we may have here a natural event described in a supernatural way. A paralytic was

* St. John v. 6-9.

healed and took up his bed and walked. How could this have happened, supposing the cure to be authentic? What natural or ordinary process may be postulated to account for it? Supposing the man was cured, what room is there for exaggeration in the account given of his cure? Positively none. We are thus driven finally to ask ourselves the question, Did Christ actually heal the man in the way described by the Evangelist? Was it so that the man looked up to this wondrous Presence, fell under the influence of His mysterious personal power, and when the command came to him sudden, sharp, irresistible, "Take up thy bed and walk," he could not choose but obey? Was it an instance of a commanding mind acting on another mind in such a way as thereby to make a decrepit body do its will? We have had no experience in these later days of any occurrence exactly resembling this. But why should we therefore say that it could not have happened? That mind can exercise an extraordinary influence over mind we have sufficient proofs. That the mind can force the body to do what no ordinary medical skill can, is equally certain. Why then may we not reasonably suppose that Jesus may have healed the paralytic in the manner described by the Evangelist? Nay, when we weigh all the evidence for and against the historical truth of the story, do we not find that this is the easiest assumption by which it can be accounted for; does it not do less violence to the imagination than any other?

A circumstance that favours this comparison between

the method in which Christ wrought His wonderful cures, and our experience of the power of mind over body, is the frequent mention in such narratives of the establishment of a suitable mental communication between Christ and the patient, prior to the consummation of the cure. In the case that has already been cited, it is left to be understood from the man's bearing towards Christ that he was capable of being brought under the healing spell. But in many other cases it is pointedly mentioned that such and such a person had "faith to be healed." The absence of such faith, it is more than once hinted, made it impossible that Christ could work His marvellous cures,—the "faith," be it understood, indicating not merely the readiness to submit the will, the temperamental aptitude for being a "subject," to use the phraseology of mesmerism or spiritualism, but, more especially, a moral qualification, there always being a mysterious connection in the cures wrought by Christ between the remission of moral guilt and the release from physical infirmity. Thus, in the account of the visit to Nazareth it is said, "And He could there do no mighty work, save that He laid His hands upon a few sick folk, and healed them. And He marvelled because of their unbelief." *

So far there is nothing of a distinctively supernatural character that we have noted in Christ's miracles of healing, nothing that appears like a violent interference with the laws of nature, which is the old-fashioned and

* St. Mark vi. 5, 6.

still perhaps common notion of the miraculous. On the contrary we have traced various points of similarity between these events described as miraculous, and events of exceptional though natural occurrence now; for the force exerted by mind over body cannot be called supernatural. Though we know so little about it, it acts, or may be conceived to act, in complete accordance with natural law. And it is to be particularly observed that all Christ's miracles of healing are of such a character that they can be conceived as having been effected in a natural though extraordinary way. For example, we never hear of His restoring an amputated limb or doing anything like a creative work. Such cures as are attributed to Him are by no means of a sort to excite justly the antagonism of medical science. They are all conceivable to those who can imagine that Christ may have possessed to a remarkable degree a curative force capable of acting on the springs of life in a diseased person.

The whole matter then hinges on the question, whether Christ may be reasonably supposed to have possessed such a power. The only way to form a proper judgment on that point is to find out as exactly as possible what sort of a person He was. And for that purpose it is necessary that we should make a close and impartial investigation of His recorded words. First of all, there is the necessity of ascertaining as correctly as possible what Christ actually did say, and then His words, all of them, not a few, should be patiently and reverentially read and re-read till they reveal their secret about the nature of Him Who spoke them. Above all, we must approach the study with an unprejudiced mind. If we take up the Gospel with a determined conviction that miracles do not happen, we shall see in them what we have eyes to see and nothing more—a Christ Who does not differ very remarkably from other good men and moral teachers. But if we set the thought of the possibility or impossibility of the miraculous aside for the time being, endeavouring to keep an open mind on the question, then we shall be in a position to judge whether Christ was such a very remarkable personage in other respects that He might well be supposed capable of doing the "mighty works" that have been attributed to Him.

After all, it is the words of Christ that exhibit most convincingly what sort of a person He was. It is by His words that, on His own acknowledgment, His personal claims must chiefly be tested. The intrinsic superiority of such a kind of evidence is manifest, especially in an age when intricate matters of history and criticism beset the recognition of the authenticity of His signs. It is an evidence, moreover, which appeals to the whole man, to the highest part of man, his conscience and his moral emotions as well as to his intellect. Yet it is not a kind of evidence that can be dealt with offhand. It cannot be passed in review and decided upon by the immediate effect which it produces. The words of Christ must above all things, so He taught, be tested by their application to the life of the person who studies them. If we would know the greatness of them, the wonder of them, we must act upon them. Christ expressly declared that it was only by a continuous practice of His teaching that men could judge precisely about Him and them. "If ye abide in My words, ye shall know the truth."* Hence it is beyond reasonable dispute, that, until a man has diligently studied the words of Christ, and reverently and obediently endeavoured day by day to fit his life to these words, he is not qualified to pronounce finally about what Christ actually was, and what He could or could not do. If this important matter of the credibility of the Gospel miracles is to be satisfactorily decided, it is indispensable, according to all the rules of just and candid criticism, that the conditions should be fulfilled, by which only, on Christ's repeated and emphatic declaration, the nature of His personality can be apprehended. It must therefore be required, that everyone who desires to have his opinion regarded concerning the capabilities of Christ, shall be able to say that he has tried for a sufficient length of time to adapt his life entirely to the teaching of Christ, that he has set before himself only the hopes and aims that Christ recommended, that he has earnestly and perseveringly endeavoured to act upon those most original and distinctive sayings, "Lay not up for yourselves treasures upon earth, but lay up for yourselves treasures in heaven," "Be not anxious for your life, what ye shall eat, or what ye shall drink, etc.," " Seek ye first the Kingdom of God, and His righteousness," "Ask and

* St. John viii. 31, 32.

it shall be given you : seek and ye shall find : knock and it shall be opened unto you," "He that findeth his life shall lose it, and he that loseth his life for My sake shall find it." When a man has experimented on the words of Christ by acting thus for a while on his theory of human life and of the highest good, then, and not till then, has he a right to be listened to with deference, when he expresses an opinion as to whether Christ was or was not such a remarkable personage, that He might well be supposed capable of healing a paralytic by an authoritative word.

The fact is, if Christ possessed any power that was distinctively original, extraordinary, miraculous, it was His power over men's spirits, their wills, their conduct, and their characters. It is to be regretted that we have been accustomed to apply this term miraculous, meaning something beyond ordinary experience, only to that kind of influence which Christ exerted over men's bodies. In reality, there are other works attributed to Him, which nobody has called in question, and yet which, to those who have had much to do with moral education, are at least equally marvellous. How hard it is to reclaim one intemperate person from his besetting vice, to win back one covetous and dishonest person to ways of honesty and self-denial! There are many who argue, that, after a character has once become firmly set, it is impossible to change it; and it must be admitted that so few are the instances of radical changes for the better taking place in men of middle or advanced age, that there is just as much ground for saying that matured characters cannot be changed, as that "miracles do not happen." In fact, a complete change of character effected in a moment of time, an instantaneous conversion, is a miracle, as much as a sudden arrestation of disease. We hear of instantaneous conversions, just as we hear of modern miracles, and we are sceptical whenever we hear of them: for most of the cases of the sort that we have been able to test have been found to be not authentic. Yet we read of instantaneous conversions in the life of Christ, and they are not supposed to present any great difficulty; nobody has taken pains to deny them, and indeed it is quite conceded that Christ was able to bring them about. Yet how can we reasonably accept this class of works attributed to Him and not the other? Christ Himself saw no distinction of difficulty between them. "Whether is easier," He asked, "to say, Thy sins are forgiven thee; or to say, Arise and walk?" Whether is easier, to free a man from his sinfulness of soul, or from his disease of body? We cannot say that the former is the easier. And therefore, if we are constrained to believe that Christ succeeded in performing miracles of healing over men's souls, we cannot reasonably dispute His power of working miracles on their bodies. What a remarkable exhibition of power was it that He made when He encountered Zacchæus! What a miraculous influence He exerted over that man, when He forced him to say in the truest language of repentance, "Behold, Lord, the half of my goods I give to the poor: and if I have wrongfully exacted aught of any man, I restore fourfold!" Have we any reason for thinking that such a manifestation of power was less remarkable than that which produced the result on the paralytic that "straightway the man was made whole, and took up his bed and walked"? It is really only our ignorance of the laws of mental and spiritual influence that makes us hesitate at all about attributing to Christ the ability to work the one kind of miracles as easily as the other. When, however, we have felt constrained to acknowledge the possession by Christ of such a power, then not only will that hesitation vanish, but we shall feel that the extraordinary thing would have been had He not exerted any miraculous influence over diseases of the body, such as He exerted over diseases of the mind. The so-called miracles of the Gospel will then fall into their proper place and have their distinctive evidential value, not as demonstrating *a fortiori* that He Who had thus power to cure the body has power to save the soul, but as affording a secondary testimony that He, Who can yet by His life-giving words turn a sinner into a saint, showed Himself while on earth to be in every respect the remarkable personage that we should have expected Him to have been, that He had power over all manifestations of life whether of soul or body.

After what has been said, it will be needless to examine further into the different classes of miracles of healing attributed to Christ, and to notice His various methods of dealing with different persons who were afflicted with disease ; how some He touched, like the lepers, as though He thereby communicated His healing "virtue" to them ; how of some He required evidences of "faith;" and how some He healed, who from their peculiar crcumstances were unable to give any such evidences. When once we are convinced that He possessed such a power of healing, it matters little to our recognition of the authenticity of these different records how He exercised it. One and all are equally probable.

But we read of other acts attributed to Him which are of a very different kind. He is not simply represented as giving sight to the blind and making the lame to walk, but as causing a legion of devils to pass into a herd of swine, as stilling a tempest, as multiplying loaves, as blasting a fig-tree, and as restoring the dead to life. In dealing with this class of miracles, we can hardly feel ourselves to be on ground so critically safe, as when we are dealing with the preceding. We cannot be so sure, that the Evangelists, in relating some of these, may not have been led to give a supernatural colouring to occurrences that happened in a natural way. For example, the herd of swine might have been seized with a panic. Instead of Christ intervening to procure their destruction, we can imagine that the shrieks of the maniacs, whom He restored to their right minds, might have had the effect of terrifying the swine, and driving them wildly over the brow of the cliff. Such an accompaniment of a notable work of healing, when it came to be related afterwards, might easily have been quoted as affording additional evidence of the manifestation of power which Christ then made.

But the same sort of explanation can hardly be suggested to account for the narrative of the blasting of the fig-tree, and of the raising of Lazarus. Both accounts are too circumstantial to be so treated, and when they are read with special reference to the explanation which Christ Himself gave of them, and to the teaching which He founded upon them, it becomes exceedingly difficult to imagine how they could have been manufactured, or described miraculously by a mistake. They force us back on to the question, whether the Christ, Who gave such evidences of an unexampled power over the whole moral and physical nature of man, could not have found it possible even to restore life to a body from which it seemed to have departed, as well as to arrest the flow of life in a plant. True, these two miracles are far more difficult to imagine as possible than any of the ordinary works of healing. There is a marked difference between increasing the vitality which already exists in a body, and restoring a vitality which apparently has left it. But though we have absolutely no experience of such a restoration of vitality, yet when we have formed such a conception of the unique power of Christ, as we cannot fail to derive from a proper study of His teaching and influence, it ceases to be difficult to imagine that He could actually have brought the dead to life. At any rate, let the narrative of the raising of Lazarus be carefully and reverentially studied *after* the endeavour has been made to obtain a right picture in the mind of the true Christ of the Gospels, and it will be easier to believe that He actually wrought the miracle, than that a narrative so dramatically perfect and so simply truthful in appearance can be other than the record of a real event. The blasting of the fig-tree again is a wonder-work of so great magnitude that the narration of it may well excite in us the surprise that the event as recorded is said to have awakened in the minds of those who witnessed it; but we have no right to deny the possibility of it till we have experienced to the full the potency of the force by means of which Christ is said to have explained the occurrence. "And when the disciples saw it they marvelled, saying, How did the fig-tree immediately wither away? And Jesus answered and said unto them, Verily, I say unto you, If ye have faith and doubt not, ye shall not only do what is done to the fig-tree, but even if ye shall say unto this mountain, Be thou taken up, and cast into the sea, it shall be done; and all things whatsoever ye shall ask in prayer, believing, ye shall receive."* What is faith? What cannot faith do?—such faith as, according to the acknowledgment of Carlyle, has done all the good that has ever been done on the earth. Faith, like that of the saints, is, we know certainly, the most powerful factor in the moral world; why should it not have power in the natural world as well? This will-force of man which acts perceptibly on his fellows, when it is intensified by a realization of the Infinite

* St. Matthew xxi. 20-22.

Invisible Being, and strengthened by a conscious communication with and dependence on that Being, why should it not be able to operate on those other forces which also emanate from the Infinite Being? At least we must confess that no one has ever given such evidence of a conscious communication with the Unseen as Jesus Christ, and therefore, till we have had experience of a power of faith equal to that which He exhibited, we cannot, even when viewing the matter in the dryest light of science, deny that He could have caused a fig-tree to wither away.

It is perhaps because in these later days we have less knowledge of the power of faith, and fewer and feebler exhibitions of it are given to the world, that we find such great difficulty in understanding how it can "move mountains." Perchance, in the future, we may be witnesses of incontestable operations of faith, similar to, if feebler than, those attributed to Christ; and then we shall be in a better position to pass a judgment concerning the mightiest and the most wonderful of the works which He is said to have performed.

Meanwhile, it is for those who profess to adhere closely to the most correctly scientific method in the investigation of truth to guard themselves from making any dogmatic assertions as to the impossibility of such occurrences. If there is wanting in favour of many of them such evidence as should rightly convince any scientifically trained mind, at least they cannot be disproved; while some of them, such as those works that have been more particularly referred to, have been rendered by recent collateral evidence in the highest degree probable. Until we are in possession of more adequate data for sifting the claims to belief of the other miracles attributed to Christ, it behoves everyone to maintain at least an open mind with respect to them.

Especially is this the case with respect to the greatest of all the miracles, that of the Resurrection. It cannot be rightly claimed in favour of that miracle that the evidence for it, strong though it may be, is sufficient to manifestly overpower the weighty arguments that may be urged against it; still less can it be rightly maintained that the rejection of that evidence as insufficient argues moral obliquity on the part of the doubter. The question of the verbal accuracy of the account of Christ's Resurrection which is given in the Gospels, is a question of historical fact, to be decided as all other such questions are decided, by evidence.* If the evidence for the miracle as recorded

* Of course it may be argued—it *is* argued, we know, by the old school of Christian apologists—that, because Jesus Christ is " God," therefore it is easy to believe that He rose again, indeed it would be strange if He had not risen again. That may be so, but it is an argument which has no scientific weight, for it is based on a statement which is not self-evident, and therefore it can carry no conviction to a scientifically trained mind. It is not in accordance with the method of reasoning which proceeds from the known to the unknown, and consequently it has not even been alluded to in the text. It is worth while remarking, by the way, that the argument has no Scriptural authority. Christ did not teach His divinity to the multitude, nor did His disciples induce their converts to believe that He rose again, by first making them believe in His divinity. The Resurrection was then as now merely a question of evidence.

is such as not to satisfy, or give certainty to, an honest enquirer, then no fault can be found with him on that account.

Any attempt to sift that evidence would be quite beyond the scope of the present work. It is doubtful whether it could be sifted now in such a way as to present a conclusion, that all honest and properly qualified enquirers would be compelled to agree with entirely. Certainly, no review of the evidence has been made as yet, that is calculated to give entire satisfaction to persons who are anxious to find out the bare truth of the matter, irrespective of any theories as to the antecedent probability or improbability of the miraculous. The existing "Lives" of Christ are for the most part written either with such a bias against the miraculous, or with such a leaning towards the verbal infallibility of the Evangelists, that they cannot carry absolute conviction to a really impartial mind. Whether a succeeding generation may be afforded the boon of a re-reading of the Gospel narrative, in the composition of which the reverence for spiritual truth which characterizes the Englishman will be happily blended with the patience and open-mindedness in investigating historical truth that characterizes the German, with a result that will be satisfactory to all, it is useless to speculate, though it may be hoped.

For the present there need be little, if any, loss from the difficulty which some feel to decide for themselves as to whether Christ did actually rise again in the manner in which He is said in the Gospels to have risen. Whatever result a correct criticism of the details there narrated may lead to, of this there can be no doubt to any who hold the beliefs set forth in the two preceding chapters, that Jesus still lives. He did " rise again," though we may not be sure how. The whole weight of the argument for the immortality of man in general tells in favour of the indestructibility of that life. Christ could not have utterly perished on Calvary. The purest and noblest career that this earth has ever been the scene of could not have been cut off finally by that brutal Jewish mob. We dare not think it, for if we do, we reject all hope of our own continuance of life after death, and all belief in a just, not to speak of a loving, God; nay we are convicted to ourselves of sin if we think it, for we falsify and reject that very witness within us which comes, as we are fain to believe, from God Himself, and which tells us that He could not have "left that Holy One to see corruption." We dare not and cannot think it; nor have any thorough believers in the religion of Christ ever dared or been able to think it. The testimony of the Christian Church in favour of the Resurrection of Christ has always been confident and clear. It could not have been otherwise. Doubtless it has been mixed up hitherto, rightly or wrongly, with an implicit reliance on the accuracy of the verbal details of the Gospel story; but that has been, properly speaking, an accident of the belief; its substance has been supplied by the deep conviction which all true Christians have felt, that it was God's will that Christ should rise again, or, more accurately, should continue to live after He "gave up the ghost" on Calvary.

Nay, that belief of the Church is a powerful witness of the fact of the "Resurrection," in addition to that which our own faith in God supplies. It is unquestionable that it has exercised an incalculably strengthening and sanctifying influence upon those who have held it, and has been a mighty factor for good to the world at large. Christians would have hitherto done little or nothing to ameliorate the world, if they had not believed in a "Risen Lord." Is it conceivable that that belief has been at heart a lie, that a conviction so deeply rooted in the minds of good men, and so fruitful in good results, can have been but a delusion continued through the centuries up till now? Not so: the so-called authority of the Church has weight in this matter; it has weight like that which pertains to the authority of our own consciences, for it is but the expression of the voice of God conveying the same testimony to a number of individual men. It may not be quoted as infallibly deciding points of historical detail, which do not fall within the province of spiritual communication; but as testimony to a religious fact it is a valuable enforcement of the testimony which is supplied by our own inward monitions of what is right and true.

It is thus then, that we may and should think of the Founder of the Christian Religion, as One Who "liveth, and was dead, and is alive for evermore." We need not attempt or even desire to penetrate the mystery, that for many hangs over the records of the Resurrection and Ascension. Whether those records are literally accurate or not, is not indeed a matter of intrinsic importance to us. We may be content to be as ignorant on the subject as we are necessarily content to be ignorant of the nature of our own translation to that life after death, which we believe is in store for us. If we cannot feel quite certain that we have an absolutely reliable report of the manner of Christ's Resurrection, at any rate we can believe " from our hearts " that God hath raised Him from the dead.* If we cannot penetrate the cloud that obscured Him from the view of His first disciples when He was "taken from them," and if we cannot adapt our thought exactly to the anthropomorphic language in which He is spoken of, as now "seated at the right hand of God the Father Almighty," we can yet assuredly think of Him as truly "ascended" to that place or state of blessedness to which we hope to be translated hereafter, and as partaking in that place or state of the highest exaltation to which perfect humanity can attain.

It is such a thought of Jesus Christ that makes Him not only the "Author" but the "Finisher" of our faith; not only the Light and Guide of our religious life; but our Forerunner, Example, and Companion in those experiences which we must pass through, if we are to attain that blessedness which we

* Romans x. 9.

believe is His now."* It is by believing in Him as One Who "died and rose again," that we are enabled truly to "die to sin and to rise again unto righteousness;" and it is by looking up to Him as One Who has "ascended into the heavens," that we may find the impulse and the power even now "in heart and mind thither to ascend, and with Him to continually dwell."

* Cf. Pascal—"C'est un des grands principes du Christianisme que tout ce qui est arrivé à Jesus-Christ doit se passer dans l'âme at dans le corps de chaque Chrétien."

CHAPTER V.

WORSHIP.

WORSHIP is the first part of religion. As soon as primitive man became conscious of the existence of some power or powers outside himself, which aroused in him feelings of awe and dependence, he was actuated by the impulse to acknowledge the relation in which he stood to those powers by presenting to them gifts, or addressing them in words, with the object of propitiating them. Since then it has always been understood that the first duty of man towards the gods, or towards God, is that of worship, the acknowledgment of their or His worth-ship. Indeed, by all in early days worship was regarded as the whole of religion, and by very many even now, if we may judge from their actions, it is still so regarded; so deeply implanted in human nature is the tendency, as Bishop Butler has phrased it, to " place the stress of religion anywhere rather than upon virtue." Worship is not of course by any means the whole of religion. Virtue or obedience to God is an essential part of it, even more essential than worship, we might say, if it were conceivable that there could be obedience to God without any recognition of His worth-ship or claims to obedience. Still worship is the first part of religion, even when religion has reached the most advanced state ; and, therefore, after a scientific investigation has been made of the facts relating to the nature of God and the methods by which His will is made known to men, the next question that suggests itself for similar investigation is, What is the scientific basis of worship?

It stands to reason that men's notions concerning worship will correspond very closely to their notions concerning God. The way in which they will acknowledge His worth-ship will depend on their conception of what His worth-ship is. The lower the thoughts they have of God the lower and meaner will be the kind of worship they will offer Him ; and any advance in the idea of God will be necessarily accompanied by a corresponding advance in the idea of worship. We note frequent illustrations of this in the history of the development of religion that is given in the Old Testament. The God of Noah was conceived to be a spiritualized man, with human, and indeed very fleshly, habits and appetites. Therefore it was supposed that He was gratified with the sweet savour of the cooked meat that was offered to Him in sacrifice. The God of the prophets, the God of Isaiah and Jeremiah, was far superior in every respect to this early object of worship. He was no longer the invisible man, powerful and dreaded, who attached himself to different individuals and furthered their fortunes, no longer even the tribal God of Israel Who delighted in victory and the blood of the slain, He was essentially a spiritual being with advanced moral attributes, Who cared not for "burnt offerings," but desired the sacrifice of "a broken and a contrite heart."

Even in the history of the Christian Church there are striking illustrations to be noted of the close relation between degraded and trivial forms of worship and a low apprehension of theological truth. Thus we find prevailing extensively in the Greek Church, and among the most ignorant in the Roman Church, the belief that God is pleased when men go on pilgrimages to sacred places, or offer candles to be burnt at His altars. Very evidently such a belief is a natural outcome of a conception of the Divine nature not much superior to that which was held by those, who thought that God was such an One that He delighted in the sweet savour of a sacrifice, and was pleased when men made vows to do Him honour. But even in more enlightened Christian circles there lingers a conception of worship which is demonstrably erroneous. If in such circles the right kind of worship, for the most part, is offered to God, it is offered not unfrequently with a wrong notion of the reasons why it should be offered, and that, of course, because a wrong notion is entertained of the Divine character. It is supposed, for example, that God delights in prayers and praises, just as He was formerly supposed to delight in burnt offerings and sacrifices, and that He is pleased to be told how good He is, just as formerly He was supposed to be pleased with the odour of a roasted kid or lamb.

In a word, if He has not now a fleshly appetite for dainty food, He has an appetite, and a very human one in the lowest sense, for praise.

That opinion is still held probably by a very large number of Christians, who are otherwise exceedingly well-informed, and it affords a proof of the curious survival down to the present time of the conception of God which prevailed among the Jews in the time of Christ. That conception had its origin in the comparison of God to the autocratic sovereigns with whom the ancient, and especially the Eastern world, was so familiar. In trying to compass the vast thought of an Almighty Ruler of all, men in those days unconsciously, and indeed unavoidably, likened Him in their minds to those earthly sovereigns who afforded them their highest experience of power and dominion. He seemed to them to resemble those sovereigns in being absolute in His rule, and in being able to exercise all authority throughout His kingdom of the world. Like an earthly potentate He—to quote the language of one of them, Nebuchadnezzar, to whom such language very naturally occurred—" did according to His will in the army of heaven and among the inhabitants of the earth; so that none could stay His hand or say unto Him, ' What doest thou ? ' "* Men in those days approached an earthly sovereign in much the same way that they approached the Almighty God, viz., with prostrations and all the gestures of reverence; and indeed the parallelism went so far that divine honours were not unfre-

* Daniel iv. 35.

quently paid to the earthly ruler, to the " Great King " or the Cæsar.

It is not surprising, therefore, that men should have conceived that the Almighty God was like an earthly ruler in this, that He desired and delighted in the homage of His subjects, and that He, as naturally as did a Nebuchadnezzar or a Nero, looked for praise and all the outward signs of submission to His authority. Now, natural and even perhaps inevitable as it was in those days to entertain such a thought concerning the Divine Being, it is nevertheless strange that that thought should have lingered so long, and should be still so extensively entertained even at the present day. For it is plainly contradictory to Christ's teaching concerning God. Christians have always held that the character of Christ was the Divine character exhibited in a human life; they have believed that Christ "revealed" God in a way in which He is not clearly revealed in Nature, by showing that He is merciful, loving, and compassionate; yet, strange to say, hitherto they have very generally hesitated to attribute to God what is perhaps the most conspicuous feature in the character of Christ, viz., His humility. Christ said of Himself, " Learn of Me, for I am meek and lowly in heart," * and men have so learnt of Him; but though He also said, " I and My Father are one "—in "heart" as in other things—they have not learnt of God the Father that He is " meek and lowly." They have continued, with a quite remarkable blindness, to regard

* St. Matthew xi. 29.

Him as inferior in this respect not only to Christ, but to good men who themselves are manifestly inferior to Christ, for they have conceived of Him as delighting in the praises of His greatness and goodness which are sent up weekly from thousands of lips; whereas it is the distinguishing mark of all good men that they do not like to have their goodness openly acknowledged, and feel abashed and ashamed when they are praised.

Plainly, therefore, if it was a true conclusion that we arrived at,* that we learn of the Invisible Power from the testimony that is derived from the highest and noblest of His works—man, as well as from our own inward intimations of what is good and true, we cannot but recognize that it is an error, and a gross one, to conceive of Him as delighting in praise.

It may be added, that what we learn concerning God from the study of Nature tends to fortify us in this judgment. If there is one thing more than another that modern writers on physical science have insisted upon, it is the way in which God hides Himself behind His works. Their investigations have not, as we have seen, tended to remove God from the universe. On the contrary, the ablest exponents of the evolution philosophy have maintained, in language that has been quoted, that He is the only, the ultimate Reality. Yet in the same breath they have passionately affirmed, that His nature is most mysterious, that though traces of His energy are everywhere visible, Himself we cannot see, and even cannot know. They have gone too far in

* Chapter II.

affirming this; they have attached excessive, even exclusive, importance to the kind of knowledge concerning God which is derived from the study of Nature; they have failed to see a revelation of God in perfect humanity, as well as in the rational universe. Still their testimony to the mysteriousness of the Invisible Power is true and valuable. It suggests a conception of God which exactly harmonises with the thought of His absolute humility as it is revealed in Jesus Christ. Had He been the haughty arrogant potentate that men were wont to think Him, we might conjecture that He would have ensured, that His power and dignity would have been so plainly manifested to men, that they would have been constrained to offer Him everywhere the adulation and the avowals of submission in which He took delight. As it is, we cannot but think of Him as One Who delights more in giving than in receiving, Who willingly hides Himself behind His works, and Who takes ceaseless pleasure in diffusing His power, His love, His sweetness, and His beauty over all, upon all, and through all, without regard to any recognition that may be made of His bounty—a truth, indeed, that is affirmed in the words of Jesus, " He maketh His sun to rise on the evil and on the good, and sendeth rain on the just, and on the unjust."

If it be true that we have no ground for conceiving that God desires our praise, the question may be asked, Why then should we offer Him our praise at all? The answer is an obvious one. For the same reason that we express gratitude to one another. If any person of our acquaintance were continually loading us with benefits, whether we deserved them at his hands or not, if he were incessantly exerting himself on our behalf in such a way as to lighten and gladden our whole lives, and yet desired no return at our hands, should we therefore accept all his favours as a matter of course, and make no acknowledgment of our obligation to him? We should think ourselves inexpressibly mean if we did so. And so we might well think it a mean thing for us to enjoy the blessings that we daily receive from the Invisible Supreme Power, and not to shew in a proper way our sense of His goodness and of our dependence on Him. Nay, just as right-thinking men are all the more eager to thank those who do good to them "hoping for nothing in return," so ought we, in conceiving of God as the infinitely Humble Being, to be all the more eager to offer Him the praise that is His due.

This then is the basis of the obligation of worship. It is founded not on the arrogant demands of a God Who is less rather than more humble than the best of men, but on what it is reasonable and proper for us to spontaneously offer Him, in acknowledgment of the benefits that we receive at His hands. Even though He does not ask us to thank Him for His benefits, it eminently becomes us to do so. Nay, in this aspect of it as a voluntary expression of our sense of God's goodness and of our dependence on Him, worship is seen to be most emphatically due from us to God. As it is expressed in the preface to the Ter Sanctus in the

WORSHIP.

Communion Office, "It is very meet, right, and our bounden duty, that we should at all times, and in all places, give thanks unto Thee, O Lord, Holy Father, Almighty, Everlasting God."

It is very important thus to establish firmly the principle upon which the obligation of worship rests, for it is only by attention to this principle that we shall avoid mistaking the kind of worship that we should offer. Manifestly our conception of the right method of worshipping God will not be the same, if we deem that He desires and demands our praise for His own satisfaction, as it will be if we regard it as a spontaneous offering on our part, becoming to us though not required by Him. Viewing worship in this latter light we cannot imagine for a moment that the *form* of our worship can be anything but secondary. The essence of worship consists in feeling, in the inward sense of the Divine worth-ship; and the expression of that feeling, the acknowledgment of the Divine worth-ship, cannot be rightly regarded as identifiable with any particular form of vocal utterance or of personal attitude or gesture. We need words and bodily signs to express our feelings to one another, but we do not need words or signs of any description to express our feelings to God. "God is a Spirit, and they that worship Him must worship Him in spirit and in truth," * is the great saying of Jesus, in which He laid down once for all the essential principle of true worship; and acting strictly on that principle we may be offering the highest worship of which we are capable, when we are

* St. John iv. 24.

holding solitary converse with God, as Christ frequently did on some lonely height, and when not a single articulate word rises to the lips, but our spirits are for the time being bowed before the Infinite Spirit in utter humility and rapt adoration. At such a time we feel that words are useless as vehicles of thought. We have passed into a region in which language is but a cumbersome expedient,* needful in our communication with one another, but a very stumbling-block in the way of our unbaring our souls before the Unseen, yet All-seeing, the Incomprehensible, yet All-comprehending Power. Unhappy are they who have never had experience of such worship in spirit and in truth; misguided,

* Cf. Coleridge, *The Pains of Sleep* :—
" Ere on my bed my limbs I lay,
It hath not been my use to pray
With moving lips on bended knees ;
But silently, by slow degrees,
My spirit I to Love compose,
In humble trust mine eye-lids close,
With reverential resignation,
No wish conceived, no thought expressed,
Only a sense of supplication ;
A sense o'er all my soul imprest
That I am weak, yet not unblest,
Since in me, round me, everywhere
Eternal strength and wisdom are."

Cf. also Wordsworth, *The Excursion*, Bk. I. :—
"In such access of mind, in such high hour
Of visitation from the living God,
Thought was not; in enjoyment it expired.
No thanks he breathed, he proffered no request;
Rapt into still communion that transcends
The imperfect offices of prayer and praise,
His mind was a thanksgiving to the power
That made him ; it was blessedness and love!"

painfully and wofully misguided, are they who do not look upon it as the very ideal worship, which, in the spiritual development of the race, we must desire and expect that men in increasing numbers will be capable of; and which we must ever keep in view in making those temporary arrangements for the outward expression of worship, which our own infirmities and the infirmities of others render necessary.

For, constituted as we are, certain forms of worship are necessary to elicit and give expression to in the minds of most, if not of all, the worship which is wholly spiritual and true. Some, indeed, who have grasped and hold firmly by the essential nature of worship as consisting of that which no words or forms can fully or sufficiently express, may be impatient of any plea even for the temporary use of words or forms. They may argue that God Himself does not value any vocal or visible expression, as such, of a spirit of gratitude and devotion to Him. They may refer to what we have seen is taught by the humility of good men concerning the Divine attitude towards praise, and may contend that the only expression of a sense of His goodness which God values, as a mere expression, apart from the feeling which He can discern without any formal exhibition of it, is that of devoted willing obedience to His commands. They may recall, that an earthly father cares far less for his child to tell him how good he is, than for him to do what he bids him; and they may maintain, that men can never so adequately express their sense of God's goodness, as when they "give up themselves to His service, and walk before Him in holiness and righteousness all their days." This would be an absolutely sound contention, for it would be founded not only on what appeals to us as thoroughly reasonable and true, but on the authority of such sayings as, "Thou desirest no sacrifice, else would I give it Thee; Thou delightest not in burnt offerings,"* and "Not everyone that saith unto Me, Lord, Lord, shall enter into the kingdom of Heaven; but he that doeth the Will of My Father which is in Heaven." †

Still, it is dangerous to fail to perceive, or to put out of mind, that even if it be only required by human infirmity, the formal and outward expression of worship is indispensably necessary to us all, inasmuch as we all are compassed with infirmity. Even if God does not value it for itself alone, we cannot do without it. It is only by the use of fixed times and seasons of prayer that we shall be kept up to the habit of prayer and praise at all, and it is only by placing ourselves in the attitude of prayer and praise, and using words expressive of our sense of obligation and dependence, that we shall for the most part feel gratitude and a desire for further Divine help. Words and sounds and sights are important instruments in stirring our emotions and moving the springs of resolve within us; and though on special occasions we can dispense with them, feeling them to be only an encumbrance and a distraction, yet on ordinary occasions, when we cannot rise unaided to the

* Psalm li. 16. † St. Matthew vii. 21.

pure and lofty height of adoration, or would be forgetful or even indisposed to make the attempt, the use of such external aids is a quite indispensable means of moving us and enabling us to offer that worship to the Infinite Spirit which is spiritual and true. We can indeed conceive of men being so entirely spiritually-minded, that for them forms are of no service and no necessity. A Moses or a Paul, we might judge, would hardly suffer if he were deprived of any opportunity of entering a house of prayer, or of expressing his sense of the worth-ship of the Infinite Power by word or sign. Such a man might be trusted to make use of the Universe as a temple, and to let Nature's marks of time, the dawn, and noon, and sunset, be his only outward mementos of prayer and praise; yet anyone else, however gifted, who was of less spiritual endowment, might possibly be risking the very existence of his Godward life, if he from a sense of self-dependence were to renounce the use of those props, which all the saints of all time have hitherto found needful to support the structure of their personal religion.

It may be, it certainly is, true, that God for His own sake does not enjoin us to worship Him with external forms; yet if for our sakes those forms be necessary, we may well say to ourselves, that then for our sakes God does enjoin them upon us, and it is a failure of duty to God to neglect them, or such of them at any rate as have been found helpful to us in the past, or have been shewn by the experience of others to be likely to help us. We may not be brought into bondage to any of them. The spiritual man has a right to assert his perfect freedom in respect to the use of particular forms of worship, and may reject those that are unserviceable to him, except in so far as his rejection of them will prove injurious to others. Whatever positive injunctions any self-governing branch of the Church or particular community of Christians may have laid down with respect to the use of forms of worship, the Christian man can boldly claim his freedom from the moral obligation to observe those injunctions, if they are not, and cannot, be made helpful to himself personally. By the rule of the Christian faith, declared in the New Testament with an insistence that cannot be mistaken, and with an authority that no collective body of Christians can override, every man who deserves to be called a Christian can claim absolute immunity from the obligation to observe any set of ordinances of human institution, which are intended to assist him in worshipping God. The Church to which he belongs can *counsel* him to observe such ordinances, but it has no moral power to compel him. For in the New Testament it is declared in unmistakeable terms and with frequent iteration that the spiritual man is free; the only responsibility that rests upon him with respect to that freedom is, that he is to use it not " for a cloke of wickedness, but as a bondservant of God." *

It has often been noticed that Jesus Christ never in any words that have come down to us, enjoined public

* 1 Peter ii. 16 (R.V.)

worship upon His followers. What He did insist upon emphatically was the necessity of private prayer, and that in terms which seem to convey that He regarded it as the chief and best means of holding communication with " our Father which is in secret." It is the utter absence of distraction in private prayer, secured by the " door closed " even to the dearest of friends and nearest of sympathizers, that gives it this pre-eminence among the means of realizing the Unseen. Still there are advantages attaching to public prayer over and above that one in which it is inferior as a devotional habit to private prayer. When men meet together for the purpose of worshipping God, even if by their company with one another they somewhat distract one another from a purely spiritual vision of God, they nevertheless render one another effectual assistance towards realizing their common relationship to God, their common dependence on God, and their common duty to God, and so the important element of brotherliness is imported into those feelings of which worship is an expression. A man who worships God only in solitude may succeed in sustaining in himself an abiding sense of God's power and goodness, and of his own dependence on and duty to God; but he is not so likely to acquire a brotherly feeling towards his fellowmen, and to be inspired to co-operate with them in brotherly work, as if in addition to his private worship he habituates himself to worship on stated occasions in company with others. We cannot achieve the best good possible to us without reference to our fellowmen.

We can only act and feel as God's children should act and feel, in proportion as we regard one another as brothers and sisters, and share one another's highest thoughts and feelings; so that it is eminently becoming to us to unite at stated times in the endeavour to recall our obligations to our common Father, and to give expression to our common desires to live in harmony with His will. Moreover, we cannot but feel, that such desires gain in purity and intensity by their being felt in common and jointly uttered; and, therefore, taking into consideration the way in which public worship enables us to realize our kinship with one another, and our duty to one another, as well as the additional strength and efficacy it gives to our common wishes for good, we cannot fail to see that there is this special blessing attaching to it, that it tends to promote a Christlike spirit among us—in fulfilment of Christ's saying, "Where two or three are gathered together in My name, there am I in the midst of them."*

It is on this ground of the way in which it suggests and promotes a solidarity among men in worship and life that the obligation of public worship mainly rests. The first thing to be thought of, of course, in worship, whether public or private, is what is due to God in respect of the recognition and acknowledgment of His worth-ship; but that which is peculiar to public as distinguished from private worship is the element of brotherliness that enters into it. It is a source of mutual help and comfort to those who take part in it;

* St. Matthew xviii. 20.

and therefore it is that in the Epistle to the Hebrews Christian people are urged to maintain the practice, in these words, "Let us consider one another to provoke unto love, and to good works, not forsaking the assembling of ourselves together, as the manner of some is, but *exhorting (or comforting)* one another."*

Besides, the public worship of God is a standing witness to the world of man's duty towards God. There can be little doubt that, if there were no such thing as public worship, if men never met together for the purpose of conjointly praising and praying to God, then the very thought of man's dependence on a Power outside himself, and of the obligation upon him of the performance of a higher order of duties than those entailed by the necessity of obeying the civil law and of rendering one's-self agreeable to one's neighbours, would not be awakened in, or at any rate kept in remembrance by, the majority of mankind. So generally has this been understood, and so abundantly has it been confirmed by universal experience, that public worship in some form or other has been an institution in every religion.

When these benefits accruing from the practice of public praise and prayer are kept in view, it is difficult to dispute the saying of Bishop Butler, that "the external worship of God is a moral duty, though no particular mode of it be so." † Yet the external worship of God can only be a moral obligation upon us in so far as that worship is calculated, if rightly participated in,

* Hebrews x. 24, 25.   † *Analogy of Religion*, Part II., Chapter 1.

to be of benefit to ourselves and to others. If the only kind of worship in which we can join, as for example when we are in a foreign country, is conducted in a manner that is unfamiliar to us and with rites that are grossly superstitious, and if in such a case our absence from worship would not be likely to set a harmful example to others, the duty of external worship cannot be said to be for the time being incumbent upon us.

The case is different when we are in our own country, and among persons whose views on religious subjects are very similar to our own, and who are likely to be more directly affected by our example. It is quite possible, of course, even at home, that we may not find any method of worship practised that is exactly adapted to our taste, or even that is incontestably rational and pure. Still, although we are not morally bound, as Bishop Butler says, to any particular form, we cannot easily exonerate ourselves from the duty to use some form—the best that is attainable by us; even though it is not our conception of the best possible. We may not favour by our countenance, if we can help it, the grossly erroneous worship of God; but it is better for us to take part in some kind of worship, which is not the best possible, and which is somewhat charged with superstition, than to live our religious lives apart from our brethren, and so run the very certain risk of becoming Pharisees in our fancied and asserted intellectual superiority to the rest of those who worship the Infinite Power; and of becoming also unloving towards them, through the loss of that stimulus to brotherly feeling and conduct which is afforded by the joint worship of a common Father. Besides, it will be very readily conjectured by those unthinking persons upon whom the obligations of religion sit very lightly, that if we absent ourselves from public worship, our absence is due not to our dissatisfaction with the forms of worship which are in use among our neighbours, but to total indifference to the duty of recognizing and acknowledging our dependence on the Infinite Power.

CHAPTER VI.

WORSHIP (Continued).

IF there are such cogent reasons, as have been suggested in the last chapter, for pressing upon all men the duty of public worship, it is evident that a very grave responsibility rests upon those who have to do with the arrangement and conduct of public worship, to see that it is devised and carried out in a way that is exactly calculated to further the ends which it is intended to subserve. It should be their care that nothing should be done in worship that is not in accordance with the highest truth ascertainable concerning the Divine nature, or that is likely to give reasonable offence to those who have approached most nearly to the intellectual and spiritual state, in which the ideal worship in spirit and in truth without the aid of form is possible.

In order to ascertain what is the manner and what are the forms of worship most likely to assist men to conjointly feel and express the worth-ship of God, regard must be had to what has apparently been proved to be beneficial by its use among the largest number of Christians and for the largest period of time. What may be called the authority of the

Church on these matters must be within reason deferred to. There is naturally a presumption in favour of forms that have been widely used from ancient times, over such as have only been recently adopted and that among isolated bodies of Christians. Still, it is quite possible, as we have abundant reason to know, and as has always been acknowledged by theologians,* that even the whole Church may err for a time, as well as particular branches of it; and therefore what may with some reason be called the authority of the Universal Church on matters of ritual and Church order has need to be carefully tested as to its right to claim our obedience. The practice of the Universal Church, or rather of the majority of Christians, for there are few practices in worship that are common to the whole Church, may suggest the form; but when the form is thus suggested, careful enquiry must be made as to whether it is in accordance with the right principles of worship, and whether it is likely to prove serviceable to the particular persons for whose use it is intended.†

To apply this rule in a few instances. It is evident in the first place that, if men and women are to meet

---

* See Vincentii Lirinensis *Commonitorium* Cap. iii., and Article XIX.

† This point is strangely overlooked by some modern writers on Worship. *E.g.*, the practical suggestiveness of some of Freeman's observations in his learned and valuable work on *The Principles of Divine Service* is frequently much impaired by his inattention to it; as for example when he expresses his opinion (Vol. I. Conclusion.) in favour of the increase of the number of Psalms to be sung at the daily services, evidently without considering whether such a change would be advantageous to the average worshipper.

together for public worship, they must provide for themselves some buildings in which they may worship. It may be said to be a practice of the Universal Church thus to provide and set apart certain buildings for the purpose of public worship. Circumstances may render it unavoidable occasionally, that worship should be conducted in places used at other times for other purposes; but, generally speaking, whenever it is possible, Christians of every school of thought prefer to worship in buildings which are used for no other purpose. Some Christians, indeed, are wont to meet together in their places of worship for other than distinctively religious purposes; and they do this not only for the sake of convenience, but also because they feel that there is cause for fear lest, in devoting a building exclusively to the purpose of worship, men and women should come to specially localize the presence of God in such a building, and deem that it is sacred as a Divine temple in a different sense from that in which the whole Universe is sacred. There is cause for such a fear, and ignorant and thoughtless people have made such a mistake. Nevertheless, the mischief arising from the mistake has never been very great, and it can always be guarded against by right instruction; while there are weighty arguments to be urged in favour of the practice of the majority of Christians of separating their places of worship from all common uses. They can plead the authority of Jesus on their side; for the propriety of consecrating certain buildings to the sole purpose of worshipping God is reasonably deducible from His saying in cleansing the temple, " My house shall be called a house of prayer, but ye have made it a den of thieves."*

Besides, it is a matter of common experience, that we are very much under the governance of the law of the association of ideas; the same sights and sounds always tend to suggest to us the same thoughts and feelings; and if a building is only used for the purpose of worship, and is always associated in our minds with that purpose, then, whenever we enter it, the thought of worship is likely to occur to us, and thus the building itself becomes an aid to devotion.

To some minds, and those not the lowest, a mountain summit, a vernal wood, a pastoral landscape, a sunlit stretch of ocean may be more immediately suggestive of worship than the most impressive building erected by man. But even such persons cannot but make a distinction, as regards the effect produced upon them, between a structure used for the common purposes of human life and one which is used as a house of prayer; and therefore for the benefit of all it is desirable to give a consecrated character to our places of worship, and to adapt them in the best manner possible to promote in those who use them such thoughts and feelings towards God as are of the essence of true prayer and praise.

Of course a great deal as regards the suitability of a building for worship—apart from the circumstance of its being reserved for that purpose only—will depend on the

* St. Matt. xxi. 13.

style of its architecture and the way in which it is fitted up. That some styles of architecture lend themselves better than others to a devotional effect is obvious, as it is also obvious that different modes of worship find each their own appropriate expression in stone, the the massive gloomy temples of the ancient Egyptians adapting themselves to the mysterious and sombre rites that characterized the worship of that people, the roomy and elaborately decorated cathedrals of Italy to the gorgeous spectacular displays which are a conspicuous feature in Roman worship, and the chaste and severe beauty of our English Gothic Cathedrals to the sober yet stately ritual of the English Church. Just as the kind of worship offered varies with the conception of the Divine nature, so the building varies with the worship; and, just as different kinds of worship are superior or inferior to one another in proportion to the relative superiority or inferiority of the conception of the Divine nature to which they correspond, so there must be a relative scale of styles of religious architecture more or less fitted to the worship which is wholly spiritual and true. That the English Gothic is the best that has been devised hitherto, it is perhaps natural that we English should think; but except we believe that the mediæval mode of worship or the modern purified mediæval is absolutely the best and not to be improved upon, no matter what further advance may be made in the knowledge of God, we cannot think that the Gothic style of architecture is absolutely the best attainable, and that some other style still better adapted to the right worship of God may not yet be invented.*

It would of course be useless to expect that, even in the case of a general advance in the knowledge of God, all men everywhere should come to prefer exactly the same style of building for public worship. Even among those who have a common faith there are differences of taste and temperament, which lead them to prefer each a more or less ornate kind of building in which to worship; and it may be safe to say that, generally speaking, what each prefers is best for each. It is easy to understand how a Venetian of the Fourteenth Century should prefer a San Marco with its almost bewildering artistic wealth to the plain white-washed building that would have most readily commended itself as a place of worship to a Covenanter of the Seventeenth Century. The one lived under a sunny sky in a city of most romantic beauty, and had reached a very high stage of asthetic culture, while the other had passed his days amid the fogs and on the bare hills of Scotland, and had no culture but what he derived from the repeated study of the literature of a people like the Hebrews by whom art was never held in relatively high repute. The Venetian would have been shocked by the conventicle; it would have contrasted so grimly with what he saw in nature,

* See Victor Hugo's *Notre Dame de Paris* (Book V., chapter 2) for some excellent observations on the relation of different styles of ecclesiastical architecture to different systems of faith and worship.

K

> "The beauty and the wonder and the power,
> The shapes of things, their colours, lights and shades,"*

and would have been so repellent to his artistic sensibilities, that within it he could not have realized the Unseen, he could not have used it as a place of worship at all; while the Covenanter, from his wholly different climatic and local experiences and deficient artistic education, would have regarded the Church of San Marco as a fit abode for the Scarlet Woman, only by an abominable blasphemy to be designated a house of God.

It is impossible then to lay down any hard and fast rule as to how a building intended to be used for the purpose of worship should be fitted up. The only or chief thing to be kept in view is, that it should be of the style best adapted to the taste of the particular people for whose use it is intended. Generally speaking, a more ornate style will be preferred by the people of Southern Europe and a simpler style by those of Northern Europe. It is very evident, for example, that the rich decorations of the Churches of Italy, Spain, and a part of France, are better suited to the sensuous and emotional temperament of the Latin races than would be the comparative severity of our Northern Churches. And this throws a good deal of light on the fact that has frequently been remarked upon, that the Reformation was eagerly embraced by the Teutonic races, and made but small headway among the races who speak languages derived from the Latin. The movement in favour of the simplification of ritual

* Browning, *Fra Lippo Lippi*.

touched no sympathetic chord in the Latin races;
on the contrary it was a movement that was objectionable to their taste; while the warm support of
the movement in Germany, England, and Scandinavia
was in one aspect of it a reaction against the
enforced imposition upon the races of the North of a
style of worship which, though suited to the Southern
races, was not suited to them.

Still it is quite possible even in the North for a taste
to be developed for the more elaborate decoration of
places of worship. There are several points of affinity
between a composite race like the English, and the
warm-blooded races of the South; and increasing
contact with those races will tend to bring about an
increase of sympathy with them. There can be no
question that the greater familiarity of English people
with the great Churches of Southern Europe is having
the effect of modifying the opinion of very many in
this country with regard to the propriety of beautifying
the buildings that are set apart for the purpose of
worship. Besides, there has been a marked and general
increase of asthetic culture in England in the present
century, and this has tended to make very many people
dissatisfied with the plain and often comfortless appearance that our Churches used generally to present; it
has produced the feeling that worship should not
necessarily be associated with what is cold, and bare,
and unsightly, and it has created a demand for a style
of Church decoration and furniture correspondent as
regards the particulars of comfort and artistic propriety

to what has become common in the appointments of the home.

It cannot be maintained that this demand is a misplaced one, or at variance with the essential principles of spiritual and true worship. If the great Temple of the Universe is beautiful, and exhibits all forms and types of beauty, then it is certainly right that any building intended by man to serve as a place of worship should be beautiful too. Indeed, the more truly beautiful it is, the better will it serve as a place of worship, and lift up the mind to Him Who, in the language of His ancient worshippers, is " The Altogether Lovely." There is a great deal of ugliness of man's origination in the neighbourhood of the habitations of man, and the better a Church is adapted to make us forget for a time that ugliness, and to set before us only what is beautiful in form and colour, the more shall we be assisted to worship God as we ought, and to derive from our worship of Him that refreshment of all our higher powers that we seek. There can be no mistake made in the devotion of the best of our artistic acquisitions to the construction and embellishment of our Churches. What we do for our dwelling-houses, at least we should do for the places in which we meet together for the highest occupation possible to us. It was a right feeling which prompted David to reproach himself in that he " dwelt in an house of cedars while the ark of the covenant of the Lord remained under curtains."* There is a manifest falseness in the religion

* 1 Chron. xvii. 1.

which will permit a man to lavish his thousands on the decoration of his home, and give but niggardly for the decoration of the building which is designated the House of God. If it is a true saying that the " beautiful is as useful as the useful, perhaps more," then hardly any expenditure of treasure on a " House of God," after due provision has been made for the sick and needy, can be deemed excessive. There need be no limits to what is done in that direction so long as mere richness as distinguished from general beauty of effect is not aimed at. If only we copy Nature, and keep its standards of beauty in view, adapting the decoration of our Churches to the measure of wealth in colour that we are familiar with in our own climate and country, we cannot go wrong. Our greatest care must be to be true to Nature, to make use of no designs that are not in accordance with the principles of form that we find in Nature, and, while carefully emulating the spiritual truth and purity of the work done by the great masters of past ages, not to imitate their necessarily imperfect *technique*, by reproducing the stilted attitudes for the human figure and the errors of perspective that are noticeable in the stained glass windows and the fresco paintings of our ancient Churches. Modern art, when exercised for religious purposes, must not be restrained by a mistaken conservatism from giving to worship the best that it is in its power to bestow. We must make our Churches and all their appointments as truthfully and therefore as perfectly beautiful as we can, yet all the while remembering that this beauty is but a means to an end, and that God is not honoured by it, if it is so lavish or so inappropriate as to distract us from realizing His Presence, or if, from whatever cause, the effect it produces upon us cannot be made to harmonize with those thoughts of God, of His power, His wisdom, His majesty, His love, and His beauty, which we ought to entertain when we desire to express our sense of His worth-ship.

The authority of the Church, the authority of collective Christian opinion past and present, thus appears to guide us safely in prescribing the setting apart of special buildings for the worship of God, and their seemly and in the truest sense artistic embellishment, always considering the end which they are intended to serve. We may expect further that that authority will be deserving of deference on the subject of the arrangements for worship made within such consecrated buildings. For example, up to the last generation it was usual for the pulpit to be the chief feature in the places of worship belonging to the Church of England. It occupied a central position at the end of the nave, often entirely hiding the Holy Table from the view of those seated in the body of the Church. Now there has been a reversion in almost all Churches to the practice that prevailed before the Reformation of putting the pulpit in a comparatively unobtrusive position on one side of the Chancel, so as to leave an uninterrupted view of the Holy Table. There can be little disposition on the part of thoughtful and fair-minded people to dispute the propriety of this arrangement. It puts the ordinance of preaching in its right place among the functions of worship, and emphasizes the importance of that act of worship which is regarded by Christians as being the chief of all because it was so explicitly prescribed by Jesus Christ, and because, even more than the eloquent exhortations of man, it tends, when we fitly take part in it, to bring us into direct spiritual Communion with God in Christ.

It is an arrangement, moreover, that may be said to be primitive in its institution, as the Holy Table in our Churches is placed in the same relative position as the ark containing the sacred rolls of the Law and Prophets in the Jewish synagogues, which doubtless furnished the model of the earliest Christian places of worship; and it was adopted in all the earliest Churches of which accounts are preserved to us.* Besides, it is endorsed by the use of a considerable section of the Protestants of Germany and of Scandinavia, as well as of the whole of the Greek and Roman Churches, the Holy Table being always a conspicuous object at the end of their places of worship; so that those who argue for the propriety of making the pulpit the most conspicuous feature in the Church can only quote in their favour the practice of the non-episcopalian Christians in English speaking countries and the Calvinists on the Continent, in opposition to that of all the rest of Christendom past and present.

It cannot be said, however, that anything like the

* See Bingham, *Antiquities of the Christian Church*, Book VIII., Chap. 3.

same weight of authority can be adduced on behalf of a fashion that prevailed in the English Church before the Reformation, and that has of late been revived. Very many of those who have interested themselves in the more artistic adornment of our Churches, and the restoration in outward sign of the Holy Communion to the chief place among acts of worship, have associated with those reforms the propriety of the wearing of a gorgeous dress by the clergy during the time of the celebration of the Holy Communion and on other important occasions. The practice of the Catholic or Universal Church has been made the authority for the one alteration as for the other; but they by no means stand on the same footing. In no true sense can the wearing of gorgeous vestments by the clergy be regarded as a Catholic practice. It was not the practice, so far as we can ascertain, in the first two or three centuries, and in all probability it was one of the innovations upon primitive usage which came from the quarter of Paganism. No practice was more resolutely repudiated at the Reformation;* and its revival now is one of the most serious departures from the principles which the most enlightened of the Reformers were actuated by. One of the principal arguments quoted for its revival is that it is an evidence of the continuity of the English Church and of her status as a true branch of the Catholic Church, her clergy dressing now

* The ambiguity of the "Ornaments Rubric" cannot be quoted against this statement. *In practice* the use of gorgeous vestments was in time *everywhere* rejected in the Church of England, except in the rare cases where the cope continued to be worn, as in Cathedral Churches.

as they were wont to do before the Reformation. Now, only the unreflecting can deny that a good deal of significance is to be attached to the effect of dress, and the continuity and rightful status of the Church of England it is desirable to assert and maintain; but whether the continuity of the Church can be best proclaimed by the donning by the clergy of the now unaccustomed and outlandish garb that was worn by their predecessors in the Middle Ages is another matter. It is likely that more persons will be annoyed or simply amused by seeing the clergy so arrayed than will be edified by the teaching that the spectacle is intended to convey. If the continuity of the Church of England is a fact, the fact can be published in the ordinary way, and the proofs of it; and men will not need to be reminded of it by means of chasubles and other antique articles of dress. Men are not prone to doubt that the House of Commons, often as it has been reformed, is the same House as that which was the Lower Assembly of the Legislature in the reign of King John, even though its chief functionaries no longer wear pointed shoes or chain mail. The testimony of history puts the point beyond all doubt to educated minds. Why may not history of itself, when it is properly related, do the same for the continuity of the Church?

But it is also argued that, inasmuch as the Holy Communion is the chief service of the Church, the clergy who officiate at the service ought to wear a distinctive dress in order to indicate that it is so. The argument is an unsubstantial one. If men are rightly instructed about the Holy Communion, if they rightly endeavour to recall, when taking part in it, what it is intended to commemorate and the good it is calculated to convey, they will succeed in the endeavour, no matter how the clergy are dressed. And even if there *were* some weight in the argument, at least it does not follow that the dress need be gorgeous as well as distinctive. There can be no harm in the clergy wearing a distinctive dress on stated occasions; but if the passages in the New Testament bearing on the status of the Ministry, and pointing out the absence of self-assertion that should characterize all the followers of Christ, are deserving of obedient attention, then it must be positively wrong for the clergy to attire themselves in the fine clothes which they are bidden to condemn in others. How can a Minister of Christ get up in the pulpit and quote those admonitions about the "outward adorning of wearing of gold, and of putting on of apparel," [*] when he himself often ministers in the Church in gorgeous raiment? True, a man may wear such raiment in the lowliest spirit, as many of the Saints have done. Still, it is certain that Jesus Christ never wore any dress but that of the peasants of Palestine. It would be impossible to imagine the Jesus Who "made Himself of no reputation, and took upon Him the form of a servant," Who washed His disciples' feet, and had not where to lay His head, arraying Himself in gorgeous attire; neither could those Apostles have done so who have left us such uncompromising precepts on the subject of dress. Now the

[*] 1 Peter iii. 3.

servant is not greater than his Lord. What Jesus and His Apostles would have shrunk from doing, the clergy of the present day assuredly may not do. True, they may quote the example of the Jewish High Priest ; but the Jewish Priest was the minister of a religion that belonged to an earlier stage of development than the Christian ; and, after all, the Christian Minister is not a successor of the Jewish Priest, but of Christ and His Apostles, and of the elders and deacons of the early Christian Church.

With respect to all questions relating to the expression of praise and prayer in public worship there can be no serious difficulty of arriving at a right judgment, when attention is paid to the principles of worship set forth by Jesus Christ, as they have already been reviewed. That praise should precede prayer, and that prayer should be offered as an act of homage to God, a recognition and a memorial of God, before it is used as an instrument for the enumeration and satisfaction of our personal wants, is plainly taught in the construction of the Lord's Prayer. The practice of the majority of Christians from primitive times illustrates how this principle should be kept in view in the arrangement of a set form of prayer for common use. The English liturgy, founded as it is on ancient models and composed to a great extent of ancient materials, furnishes an irreproachable example of the order in which the thoughts which we ought to entertain with respect to the Divine Being should be successively evoked in worship, in the confession of sin, followed by praise and thanksgiving, and then supplications and intercessions. The question as to whether the use of forms of prayer is preferable to extemporary prayer in worship has so often been argued that it will not be dwelt upon here. Speaking generally, there is a predominant weight of argument and of authority in favour of the use of forms of prayer almost exclusively, though it must be acknowledged that on certain occasions and for certain classes of persons extemporary prayer may with advantage and perfect propriety be used to further the ends of united worship. Forms of prayer may be for certain purposes too general and too inelastic, while there is always the danger of their becoming in some respects antiquated and so far unreal. These defects, however, can always be remedied by the introduction into a liturgy of special prayers and thanksgivings for special occasions, and by the elimination from it of modes of expression and subjects of petition which are unsuited to modern worship. The periodical revision of a liturgy, difficult for various extraneous reasons though it be, and as in fairness it ought to be recognized by all to be, is essential to its fullest usefulness. For example, prayers drawn up in one century for the Divine guidance of the rulers of the State, ought to be altered in a later century, when power has come to be differently distributed between the different orders of rulers. When matters like this are attended to, the comprehensiveness as well as accuracy and dignity of statement of a great liturgy, make it vastly superior as a means of calling forth and expressing the devout feelings of a congregation to the necessarily much more imperfect extemporaneous utterances of even the most talented and devout minister.

An important thing to be kept in view in the regulation of public prayer according to the essential principles of worship is, that it should be adapted to retain the interest of those who take part in it. For that purpose it should be as void as possible of repetitions, and should not run to an undue length. A form of prayer, however admirable it may be in language and style, is but a means to an end—the expression of the devout feelings of those who use it; the form is made for man and not man for the form; and therefore if in some parts of it words and phrases are repeated so often that the mind cannot readily follow them, then it so far defeats its end instead of furthering it. The frequency of the use of the Lord's Prayer and of prayers for the Sovereign in the services of the English Church, especially when two or three of those services are taken together, and the reiteration of petitions for Divine grace and mercy at the conclusion of the Litany are instances in point. Of course it may be argued, that no liturgy can be so framed as to call forth and sustain the interest of those who worship, unless they set their minds intently to the task of following it, and the most concise form of prayer might often be listened to with intermittent attention. That is perfectly true. Still there should be no provocatives to inattention like undue repetitions in a form of prayer, and it must always be remembered that the greater number of persons who pray in public will with the best intentions be subject to the average human infirmities, and what might be adapted to a few earnest persons of saintly mind will not be adapted to them. The best attainable form of prayer, therefore, for public use will have this merit among others, that it will be that best calculated in point of precision and conciseness to maintain without interruption a devout train of thought in the mind of the average worshipper.

Much of what has been said with respect to the style of composition of a form of prayer, as regards the effect it is calculated to produce on those for whose benefit it is provided, will apply also to the way in which it is recited or sung. The most exceptionally composed liturgy can be so mutilated, and even desecrated, by bad reading, that it may be a positive hindrance to worship to listen to it, and it may be so tediously recited as to cause weariness, however short it may be. It is indeed a matter of extreme importance that such provision as is possible should be made for the careful, distinct, intelligent, and devout reading of a liturgy, whenever it is used. Elocution becomes an art of primary importance when upon it is made to depend the devotional effect produced by a liturgy on the largest number of those who join in it. The man who, having taken pains to make himself proficient in the art, endeavours on all occasions when he reads a form of prayer to express the exact sense of what he reads, and to read it in a frame of mind adapted to its sacred import, renders a most valuable service to religion; for the tones and the style in which he speaks are calculated in the highest degree to promote for the time being in his hearers a sense of God's worth-ship, and a desire to offer to Him their praises and prayers in sincerity and truth. It would be well if all those who have to officiate at public worship were to take care to prepare themselves beforehand for their responsible task by recollecting the aim and purpose of it, and by bearing in mind that the sacred words they have to repeat will have no value as a memorial before God unless they express the devout feelings of those who are taking part in the service, and that, in order that that result may be accomplished, they must be said in a tone and manner calculated to evoke and sustain the lively interest of those on whose behalf they are uttered. It is not by any means sufficient to remember that the words are to be spoken in the presence of God; it is just as necessary to remember that they are to be spoken in the presence of man.

In the regulation of the use of music in public worship the same attention needs to be paid to the tastes and capacities of a congregation. The question of whether and how far prayers as well as praises should be sung, is one which has reference only to the effect which is likely to be produced on the feelings of the worshippers. If it is calculated to solemnize those feelings and assist devotion by harmonizing the joint utterances, without at the same time diminishing the fervour of them, it is not only permissible but good. It never can be rightly maintained, however, that a musical recitation of a liturgy is essential to its proper performance as a memorial before God. It is a derogation from the character of the Divine Being to hold or teach, that He, being such as He is, the Infinite Being, superior in every way to the limitations of our human nature, can be pleased with the melody of sound so much as to regard it as a necessary accompaniment of the proper recognition by man of His goodness and power. That all sensuous beauty in the universe, whether of sound or form or colour, is pleasing to the Eternal Mind by Whom the universe is governed and sustained is only to be supposed; but that beauty of sound could enter at all into comparison in His judgment with the moral beauty of those feelings of gratitude and awe and love which comprise what we call adoration and thanksgiving as expressed by man—the highest and most perfect of all the creatures of God that are known to us—is a thought that it would be folly to entertain. Music, and the best of it, ought unquestionably to be adapted on occasion to the purpose of worship, even on the ground that when we express our feelings towards God by means of sounds it is becoming that we should express them in the best manner possible to us. Still, it is almost solely, if not altogether, with respect to the effect it has in eliciting devotional feeling in a congregation that music is of value in the worship of God. That music operates very powerfully on the feelings is known to all, and therefore the utmost resources of music may well be employed for the purpose of eliciting and expressing man's sense of the Divine power and goodness. There is always the fear, however, when music has come to be much employed in the service of the Church, that the fact may be lost sight of that it is a means to an end. Too often it has been forced on those who do not highly appreciate it, and to whom it is not and cannot be made a real aid to devotion; while for others it has been used on certain occasions in excessive abundance, so as to produce mental and physical fatigue. Most important is it, therefore, that the musical rendering of praises and prayers, like the ordinary reading of them, should be done always in remembrance of, and with reference to, the effect it is likely to produce on a congregation. That arrangement of Church music is the best which is not merely the most consistent with the highest canons of the musical art, but is adapted as exactly as possible to the musical capacity of those whose praises and prayers it is intended to evoke and express, and to their powers of attention and of physical endurance.

The right regulation of the use of music for the purpose of public worship is a matter of great moment at the present time. The much-increased use of music in places of worship, encouraged and furthered as it has been by the manifest approbation of those for whom it has been provided, has tended to produce in unthinking minds the opinion, that the mere listening to the utterance by a trained body of singers of sacred words set to sacred music is in itself worship; and "services," so called, of that sort have come to be attended by not a few, just as sacrifices were formerly attended, the vocal and instrumental music taking the place of the sacrificial victim as the medium for propitiating the Divine Being. It is well then that, to prevent such a flagrantly superstitious abuse of a great gift of God, it should be clearly and emphatically taught, that there can be no value at all in a musical " service," however beautiful it may be, except in so far as it is calculated to fill the hearts of those who listen to it with the feelings which it is proper for them to entertain towards God with reference to the special circumstances under which the service is held.

There are numerous other questions relating to the conduct of public worship which are capable of easy settlement when reference is thus made to the meaning of public worship and the conditions of its reality as a mode of promoting spiritual communion between man and God. It is through inattention to these things that so many ill-advised practices have been introduced into Christian worship in different parts of the world, and that so much embittered controversy has arisen over matters of intrinsically trivial importance. Over and over again insistence has been laid on certain customs as though they were absolutely essential to true worship, when a moment's unprejudiced reflection, it would have been thought, would have shown how groundless was such insistence. For example, there are very many Christians, some even in England, who think and teach, that to receive the Holy Communion after partaking of ordinary food on the same day is an abuse of that sacred ordinance. An opinion like this not only does violence to history and reason, but asperses the character of the Divine Being; for how could He be worthy of adoration if He could be supposed capable of being affected by such things? As a matter of fact, the celebration of the Holy Communion in the earliest times always followed on the *Agape*, or Love Feast, and indeed the Sacrament was first instituted "after supper." There were good reasons, no doubt, for afterwards altering the time of the celebration to early morning instead of the evening, and there are good reasons now for inviting Christians to partake of the Sacrament in the first part of the day. Moreover, it is a quite justifiable counsel to those who are young and strong that they should let the first occupation of the day be that of attendance at the Sacrament, and the first food of the day be that of the sacred feast; but in face of the testimony of history as to the original practice of receiving the Holy Communion directly after a meal, it is unwarrantable to contend that under no circumstances should food be taken before communicating. Here again, if the end and aim of the service had been kept in view, no mistake of this sort would have arisen. The Holy Communion is celebrated primarily in order that we may bring to remembrance the sacrifice of the death of Christ and the benefits that we receive thereby, and that in partaking of the consecrated Bread and Wine we may partake spiritually of the Body and Blood of Christ, that is to say, be spiritually nourished on the Spirit of Christ. Now, in order that we may derive full benefit from the service, it is necessary that we should attend to it with the full power of our minds; and the more healthy the condition our brains are in the better shall we be able to exercise that power. It is evident, therefore, that, if we go to the service with our brains in a state of exhaustion from hunger, we shall not only not be able to give our full minds to the service, but have to wrestle all the while with those tendencies to irritability and mental restlessness which we experience when our brains are in an ill-nourished state. It is not good to go to the Lord's Table in a state of repletion, but it is equally bad, as regards the character of the memorial we shall offer, and the effect the service is likely to have upon us, to go in a state of exhaustion. St. Paul's injunction,* " If any man is hungry let him eat at home," applies equally to such a case as to that of those who were wont to desecrate the Holy Communion by using it as a common meal; and the prohibition to take food before communicating, transgressing as it does the principle laid down in this injunction, is an instance of the mistakes that men will make when they are not careful to keep in mind the meaning and purposes of the ordinances of religion.

The same may be said of some other matters relating to the performance of what has always been regarded as the highest act of worship in the Christian Church. It is quite distressing to note how devout and learned men have painfully exercised their minds about certain forms of prayer or praise, or certain ceremonial acts, in

* 1 Cor. xi. 34.

the celebration of the Holy Communion, as though upon the use of these depended the "validity" of the Sacrament, as the phrase is, which can only properly mean its value as a devout commemoration of Jesus Christ, and as a means of spiritual nourishment to those who partake of it. That all things in public worship should be done "decently and in order,"* is on every ground desirable and right, and that, for the determination of what is of most propriety in the conduct of worship, the practice of the majority of Christians from the beginning of Christendom should be generally referred to, is most reasonable, as has been already argued. It cannot be said, considering the importance attaching even to small matters with respect to the securing of a decent and orderly performance of public worship, that certain so-called innovations in worship in the Church of England during the last half century have not been rightly contended for. Still, it has been a cause for grave regret that so little discrimination should have been shown between what is important and what is unimportant in worship, and that the peace of the Church should have been interrupted for the sake of the introduction of things which in themselves could be neither specially acceptable to God nor edifying to man, in apparent forgetfulness of the essential principles of the religion which was founded by Jesus Christ.

Attention to those principles must convince any unprejudiced person that the extra elaboration of

* 1 Cor. xiv. 40.

worship is on the whole a retrogressive thing. To contrive means in public worship of influencing men through the senses of sight and hearing is, as we have seen, a necessary accommodation to the nature of man ; but to multiply such means inordinately is to introduce an element of great danger into public worship, inasmuch as it tends to make it more the performance of a number of outward acts than a means of uplifting the thoughts and feelings to God. Too great a complexity of ritual is only too likely to defeat the main object of Christian worship, by keeping men's minds enslaved to sensual things, instead of assisting them to enjoy rightly that spiritual liberty which is the priceless heritage of the disciples of Christ.* The paraphernalia of worship are legitimate and truly useful only so far as they are reasonably consistent with Christ's teaching concerning God and the way He is to be approached in prayer and praise by man; and the worship of the future, in so far as it will be progressive in the best sense and not retrogressive, will tend to

* Note on this head the judicious words of the preface "Of Ceremonies" in the Prayer Book:—" What would St. Augustine have said if he had seen the ceremonies of late days used among us ; whereunto the multitude used in his time was not to be compared ? This our excessive multitude of ceremonies was so great, and many of them so dark, that they did more confound and darken than declare and set forth Christ's benefits unto us. And besides this, Christ's Gospel is not a Ceremonial Law (as much of Moses' Law was) but it is a religion to serve God, not in bondage of the figure or shadow, but in the freedom of the spirit; being content only with those ceremonies which do serve to a decent order and godly discipline, and such as be apt to stir up the dull mind of man to the remembrance of his duty to God, by some notable and special signification, whereby he might be edified."

emphasize that teaching by associating with itself more and more simple though not less dignified and beautiful forms.

That the organization of the public worship of God will take such a direction in future, after the present reaction towards elaborate traditional forms has spent itself, there is good ground to hope. It is impossible but that the scientific spirit, which is so markedly leavening the thoughts of all classes in the civilized world, will more and more assert itself in the judgments which men will form on matters theological and ecclesiastical, as well as those relating to common life. It may thus be expected, that the manifest inconsistency between the over minute and precise attention to petty details in worship, and the utter spirituality of the worship which Christ prescribed, will become in time a matter of common notoriety, and men will in increasing numbers be nourished in the belief, that to hold frequent communion in spirit with the Infinite Ruler of all, and to live in dependence on His power and goodness and in obedience to His laws, are the only absolutely indispensable conditions of rendering to Him that worship which is His due.

Appendix.

Appendix.

THE HOLY LAND AS THE THEATRE OF REVELATION.*

JUDGES XVIII. 9.

"We have seen the land, and, behold, it is very good."

T is only relatively that Palestine could ever have deserved the name in the ordinary sense of being a very good land. Its scenery is impressive, but not by any means equal in beauty to that of many parts of the British Isles. Its soil is fertile, but only in patches between the hills, and in the lowlands of the Jordan Valley and the Western plain. It is no more than a Westmoreland or a Carnarvonshire for productiveness. Yet in contrast with the deserts, terrible for their deathly sameness and sterility, that surround it, it merits all the terms of praise that are lavished upon it in the Bible; it is indeed "a land of wheat, and barley, and vines, and fig-trees, and pomegranates," "a land that floweth with milk and honey," "a land of mountains and plains, which drinketh water of the rain of heaven."

Too often those who have visited the Holy Land give unduly disparaging accounts of its scenery and resources, and too often those who read these accounts, and who look at photographic views of the country, acquire the impression that

---

* This Sermon was preached after the Author's return from a visit to the Holy Land. Although in it will be found the repetition of part of what has been already said about Revelation, it is inserted in the expectation that it will throw some additional light on a subject of which it is difficult, yet most important, to obtain a clear view.

the glowing descriptions of the Bible are overcharged. When, however, it is remembered that it is the only well-watered country, with the exception of the artificially irrigated Egypt, in a tract of many thousands of square miles of sterile rock and plain, there is no cause for surprise that those who first entered it from the wilderness of the South should have given the report of it that it was very good.

But though the Holy Land is surpassed by many other countries in those features of beauty and productiveness which suggest that epithet in the ordinary sense, it deserves it in another sense to a degree far beyond any other country on the face of the globe. If it is relatively a good land in respect of its power to nourish man's body with food, and to delight his artistic sensibilities with beauty, it is absolutely the best of all lands in its adaptability to further the development of the spiritual life of man. If it cannot, and never could, be made to bring forth such abundant harvests as the neighbouring Egypt, if it has not sufficient grace and grandeur of appearance to make it a Switzerland or a Norway, it nevertheless has the distinction above all other lands of being the one best suited to the requirements of the spiritual nature of man, and the one in which it is easiest for man to hold converse with God, and to receive from God the revelation of His mind and will.

God, we know, does not do things by accident, any more than He acts from caprice, and if one land has been the scene of all the highest communications of His will to man, it is not because He arbitrarily and without reason chose to have it so, but because that land was specially adapted to fit men for receiving those teachings which God reveals unto us by His Spirit. The circumstance which in history gives its unique interest to Palestine is, that time after time God spoke to the spirits of men there, and that with a higher message than He communicated to others elsewhere. We may not deny, of course, that He spoke to others elsewhere. He spoke to Sakya Mouni in India, to Zoroaster in Persia, to Socrates in Greece; but to neither of these three did He speak as He spoke to Him Whom we call His Son. The Light of India, and the Light of Persia, and the Light of Greece pale in the Light of the World. And, moreover, in the land which we rightly distinguish as Holy there was a succession of prophets, each as regards his insight into spiritual truth in advance of the most enlightened men of other countries, culminating in Him Who is "the very effulgence of the glory and the express image of the substance" of the Invisible God.

It is a fact of considerable significance that all the greater religions—that is to say, the religions that have had the greatest sway—have had their origin in the East. Europe with all its advantages has never been the cradle of a new faith, though it has been the best nursery of the chief of all. The common explanation of this would be, that the genius of the European races, though admirably adapted to the origination and culture of the various arts and sciences, is not suited to the reception at first hand of those truths which are communicated to men by the process which we call revelation. Doubtless this is true as far as it goes. It is impossible not to mark a fundamental difference between the temperament and cast of thought of the Eastern and Western races, as regards their way of apprehending religious truth. All the Eastern races—meaning those of India, Persia, Syria, Arabia, and North Africa—are by nature profoundly religious. Religion in them is a natural growth and not an acquisition from the outside. It shapes all their thoughts, it colours all their language, it is part and parcel of all their outer life. They are not half ashamed of it, and fearful to make any public exhibition of it, as are most Europeans. They say their prayers in public; they salute their friends in God's Name; they more often mention that Name than any other. No doubt their religion is frequently indistinguishable from the grossest superstition, and they are credulous in respect to the supernatural to a degree which at every turn excites the wonderment, and sometimes the contempt, of the far more critically-minded European. Still the fact remains, that the people of the East are fundamentally religious, in the sense that they live day by day in vivid consciousness of the Unseen.

Now, instructed as we are to associate differences of national character with differences of climate and country, we are not disposed to stop at the apprehension of the fact that the Eastern races are more naturally religious than the Western, as though it were a fact about which nothing more was to be said. We are moved to draw from it the legitimate and necessary inference, that the climatic and physical characteristics of the East are more favourable than those of the West to the cultivation of the religious instinct in man. What those climatic and physical characteristics are, it is worth our while carefully to note, in order that we may endeavour to make up for the want of them, or learn to use them duly when they are available.

Taking notice first of climate, we have to remark, that to the East and South of the Mediterranean the warmth and evenness of the temperature are such, that the wants of the body are reduced to a minimum; the inhabitants of those regions can subsist on less food than we, and do not need so much clothing to protect them from the severity of the weather. The simplest food, and that always of the same kind, suffices for them; while all the year round they can wear the one description of clothing, and that has come to be a uniform, unchanged in shape or colour, so that they need to give far less thought than we to "what they shall eat, and wherewithal they shall be clothed." Moreover, they are not required by the exigencies of the climate to take the extra precautions against cold and damp that we are. They do not need the same elaborate dwellings, with the same number and variety of rooms in them, that we do, inasmuch as they have no cause to spend so much of their time in their homes and under cover. Indeed, at certain seasons of the year it is no hardship to them to sleep under the open heavens, as David did in his youth, and as Jesus frequently did. It was more a mark of the poverty than of the severity of our Lord's life, that " He had not where to lay His head."

Now there is a triple advantage arising from these peculiarities of Oriental life. They obviate the impediments to the development of the spiritual nature which result from the necessity of paying engrossing attention to the wants of the body; they allow of more leisure for religious meditation, and "the wisdom of the learned man"—of the spiritually learned man, as of others—"cometh with the opportunity of leisure;" while they make men much more familiar with Nature in all her aspects, and more susceptible of the influences of Nature, and so bring them more nearly in contact with the Invisible Spirit, in Whom all things animate and inanimate have their being.

Of course, it cannot be said of the Oriental races generally, that they use their climatic advantages to the utmost benefit of their spiritual nature. They are not by any means now in the van of religious thought; on the contrary, their religious beliefs are far less pure than those of the Western races, and their moral practice is on the whole distinctly inferior. They have degenerated from what their forefathers were, chiefly owing to political causes, and are as much behind the Christians of Western Europe in respect of their religious beliefs, as their forefathers were in advance of the Celts and Teutons of the early days of the Christian Era.

Still the faith of the Teutonic and Celtic races, if we may make bold to say that it is now the purest in the world, is after all only a borrowed faith, a faith that had its origin in the East; and the present religious degeneracy of the Oriental races cannot affect the deductions to be drawn from the fact, that the great religions that now hold sway over so many millions of human beings all had their origin in the East.

It may be, that the modern dwellers in the East are not availing themselves for the purposes of the religious life, as others have done in the past, of the unique climatic and other natural advantages of the region which they inhabit. Still, that should not cause us to forget, that it is only by using such advantages to the full, that men have hitherto attained to the privilege of being recipients of previously unknown truth by the process which we call revelation.

How that has come about, a moment's reflection on the nature of revelation will shew. Revelation means, of course, unveiling—the making clear what before was invisible, or seen only doubtfully as through a veil. Now by men as they are ordinarily circumstanced God is not perceived. God's Spirit lies all around us, permeating all we see; yet we are unaware of the fact in our ordinary state. Even though we live and move and have our being in God, we may not be conscious of His nearness to us, and of our dependence on Him. There is only one way in which we can apprehend Him, and that is by our spirits coming in contact with His. Thus and thus only can the highest truth concerning God be made known to men. " Eye hath not seen, nor ear heard, neither have entered into the heart of man, the things which God hath prepared for them that love Him. But God hath revealed them unto us by

His Spirit." It is a most mysterious saying, but this much, at any rate, of its meaning is clear, that it is not by the exercise of the lower faculties of sight, or hearing, or reason, or imagination, that we can discover the "things of God," but only by what cannot be otherwise described than as the intercommunion of our spirits with God. The highest truth concerning God cannot be arrived at by the same processes by which other kinds of knowledge are acquired. It must be "seen" as it were with an inward eye. We must be placed in such a condition both of inward preparation and outward circumstance, that our powers of spiritual perception may be made sensible of those Divine influences which abound everywhere for those who are capable of apprehending them. So it is that all those who have proclaimed fresh truth concerning God in times past have acquired it. They have gone out "into the wilderness," or on to the hills, where nothing has interfered to prevent their realization of the all-pervading presence of God. They have there divested themselves of all but the most needful cares for the body; they have closed their eyes to earthly sights and their ears to earthly sounds; they have for the time being renounced the ever obtrusive thought of their own personality; they have been in such a condition that whether they were in the body or out of the body they could not tell; they have been conscious of nothing but God and His works; and then it is that, as they have said and believed, God has whispered His secrets to their hearts, filled their souls with His peace, and dismissed them afterwards to their task of acting as His messengers to men, with their faces irradiated, like that of Moses, with the glory of God, and their memories stored, like that of Paul, with "unspeakable" words, that it was not lawful or possible for them to utter.

So absolutely necessary is it that these conditions of entire isolation in the presence of Nature, and entire deliverance from all pressing needs of the body, should be fulfilled, not for a short space only but for a protracted period, if men are to be capable of holding such close communion with God, that we can well understand how it is only in the East, where life can be made so simple, that men have hitherto been able to receive fresh "revelations" of religious truth.*

But other than merely climatic conditions are needful to render those, who thus hold communion with the Infinite Spirit, capable of receiving God's truth in its due proportions, and in all its magnificent universality. How is it that Buddhism as a religion is so inferior to Christianity, so limited in its adaptability to the manifold wants of mankind, so defective in its representation of the dignity of human life and the lovableness of the Great Author of all? Surely one reason, and an important one is, that he, or rather they, who wrought it out, holy-minded men, as we are fain to say, had their powers of vision straitened by the limitations of the land in which they lived and of the society to which they belonged. It was a land, for the most part, flat, and tame, and bare, remote from the mysterious and vivifying influences of the sea; a land of frequently intense heat, and often refusing its products to the teeming millions that thronged it; a land darkened by the despotism of its rulers and saddened by the misery of the vast majority of its inhabitants. What wonder then that the most spiritual men in such a land were able only to declare to their fellows a creed whose

---

* This and the preceding paragraph must not be read to imply that there has been no "revelation" at all communicated to men since the early days of Christianity. The point insisted upon is, that no new truth, of which the germ at any rate is not to be found in the New Testament, has been discovered since. Poets, such as Wordsworth and Tennyson, are rightly spoken of as prophets; but their utterances have coincided with, and put into modern expression, not added to, what is to be read in the Bible.

dominant note was pessimism, a creed that, like Christianity indeed, enjoined self-renunciation, but held out no crown, if it be a crown, but that of annihilation to those who bore the Cross?

We have only to contrast Buddhism with Christianity, in order to see how all the features in Christianity, that make it the one religion for men, correspond to the unique characteristics of the Holy Land, as a theatre for a perfect revelation. In the diversity of the structure and scenery of the Holy Land, composed as it is of plain, and hill, and spring, and brook, and shore of the sea, we see the counterpart of the Divine adaptability of the Bible to the diversified wants and temperaments of all the people on the face of the globe; in the storms and earthquakes to which it is subject we see the suggestion of the just presentation in the Bible of the severer aspect of the character of God; in its lonely mountains we trace the symbols of the awful majesty and eternal self-existence of the Divine Being; in its fertile plains we see the tokens of His goodness and mercy; while the comparative tameness of the general character of its scenery tends to enhance its fitness as the cradle of a religion "which was destined to have no home on earth, least of all in its own birth-place, which has attained its full dimensions only in proportion as it has travelled further from its original source,"* which is founded on the doctrine that, albeit some lands more than others may be suited to the unveiling of God's truth, yet the service and worship of God suggested by such knowledge is independent of climate and latitude, for He is a Spirit, and they that worship Him are required only to fulfil the conditions of worshipping Him in spirit and in truth.

Thus it is, as we can partly see, that the highest knowledge that we have of God has come to us from the Holy Land.

Two brief practical reflections will give a profitable conclusion

*Stanley, *Sinai and Palestine*, ed. 1881, p. 156.

to our study of this subject. The first is, that if we would approach as nearly as we can to the condition in which it is possible for the spirit of man to come consciously into contact with the Spirit of God, we must be careful not to let the wants and desires of the body have a too engrossing share of our time and of our thought; we must not impair our powers of spiritual perception by making ourselves too dependent on material comforts and luxuries; we must remember that we cannot pamper our bodies except at the expense of our souls; plain living and high thinking are inseparable.

Our second reflection is, that though we cannot, owing to the conditions of our life in a northern latitude, spend whole nights in the open air in prayer to God, we can "enter each into his chamber and shut the door," and there have such real though transient glimpses of the King in His beauty, that the radiance of them will long remain with us to purify and gladden our lives, and to inspire us with the desire to see Him eventually as He is, in all the glory and perfection of His nature.

By the same Author.

PRESENT-DAY COUNSELS: ADDRESSED TO A MIDDLE-CLASS CONGREGATION.

Crown 8vo., 5/-.

THE SCOTTISH LEADER *says:*—"It is seldom that a volume of sermons is issued which was so well worth giving to the world. The term invigorating, perhaps, best expresses the effect produced by even a hurried perusal. . . . Whether or not the questions which Mr. Cox takes up are more pressing now than they have been, there can be no doubt that many people do want them answered, and, moreover, that they will be glad to have them answered in the spirit of strong common sense, as well as sincere religion, which this volume displays. . . . We commend Mr. Cox's book to all who can appreciate direct and manly preaching and sympathetic as well as outspoken counsel."

THE RECORD *says:*—"The sermons are in many respects admirable. They all contain sober thought, not by any means commonplace, often expressed with genuine originality. The point of view seems to be that of a moderate churchmanship, not biassed by party spirit on either side."

THE SCOTSMAN *says:*—"Their topics as well as their treatment are directed specially to the spiritual wants of the present generation, and upon such matters as the Authority of the Bible, the Relations of Science and Religion, and the like, they speak with earnestness always, and with good sense rather than eloquence."

THE LIVERPOOL MERCURY *says:*—"The volume belongs to our local literature, and certainly does it honour, the problems of the age are faced so manfully. The audience is to be congratulated that can count upon hearing sermons characterised by so much reverence, insight, and scientific boldness."

C. KEGAN PAUL & CO., LONDON.

www.ingramcontent.com/pod-product-compliance
Lightning Source LLC
Chambersburg PA
CBHW032148160426
43197CB00008B/819